EMOTIONAL REGULATION

Emotional Algorithms for Clients and Counselors

Peter Ladd

with Yasmeen Zaidi

Hamilton Books
Lanham • Boulder • New York • Toronto • Plymouth, UK

Copyright © 2018 by
Hamilton Books
4501 Forbes Boulevard
Suite 200
Lanham, Maryland 20706
Hamilton Books Acquisitions Department (301) 459-3366

Unit A, Whitacre Mews, 26-34 Stannary Street,
London SE11 4AB, United Kingdom

Library of Congress Control Number: 2017953683
ISBN: 978-0-7618-6987-0 (pbk : alk. paper)
eISBN: 978-0-7618-6988-7

⊖™ The paper used in this publication meets the minimum
requirements of American National Standard for Information
Sciences—Permanence of Paper for Printed Library Materials,
ANSI Z39.48-1992

This is dedicated to those who have the courage to face the emotions in their lives.

Contents

Figures

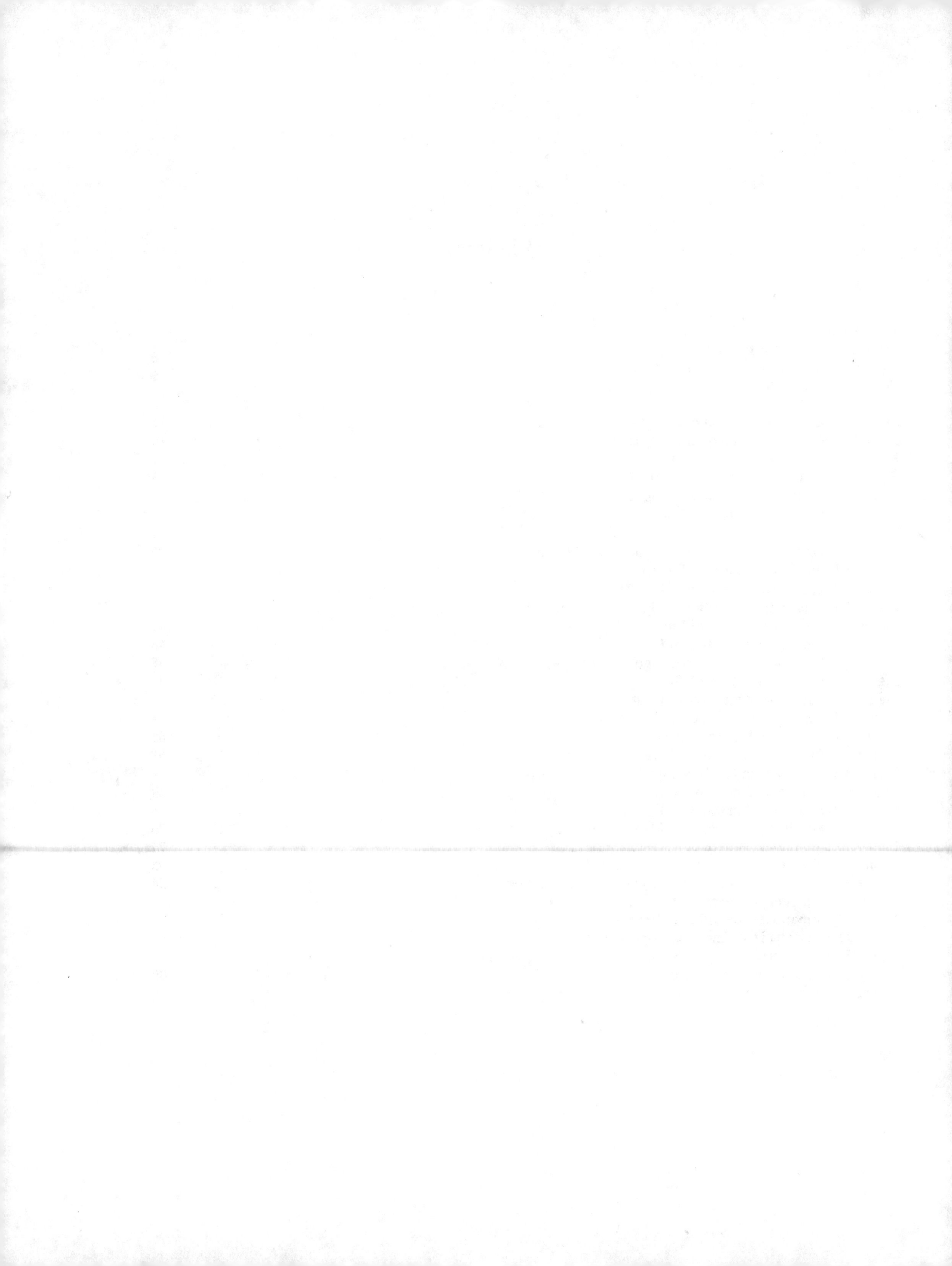

Preface

Numerous professionals have asked me to write a book that would give guidance to addiction and mental health clients, and their counselors or therapists. The following is my attempt, along with my colleague, Yasmeen Zaidi, to provide more of a reference book than a workbook, though much of what is contained in the following pages may require the reader to work through specific questions, directives, and possible therapy interactions.

My belief for many years, as a psychologist, rests in empowering clients, students and others to find their personal solutions to life problems. This becomes especially true when considering emotional regulation. So, the idea of acting as an expert in other peoples' lives regarding their emotions does not sit well with me. If I can use a metaphor to make my point, "I see myself as a stage hand in someone else's play. I am not the director or the star of the play, but the person who sets the stage for the play to go on." The star and director of the play resides in you. It is your life and it should be your direction that is taken seriously.

Therefore, this book hopefully will not be perceived as two academics telling you what to do with regulating the emotions in your life. It is designed to give you as many possibilities for your personal exploration as we could think of, along with what others have given us. Having said that, it may be important to keep in mind how you might read this book. It can be read in any number of ways. Like any other workbook, it can be read from cover to cover, while answering the questions and exercises presented to you in each chapter. However, this does not mean you *must* answer all the questions or do all the exercises, unless in a group setting or a therapy setting some professional asks you to use it in that way. *From our point of view, only those items that can help you emotionally grow and change make sense to answer.* Also, since the book is based on different emotions, it can be read by picking an emotion that you may want to explore more in-depth. Some people have used it in that manner.

Another way to read it is focusing on the emotional patterns and emotional algorithms found in each chapter and discuss them with a counselor or therapist that address specific emotional problems while skipping the questions and exercises. Or, simply pick one issue hidden in the book that you find problematic regarding your emotions and go from that point. We are hoping that it is becoming clear that Yasmeen and I are more concerned with *you* choosing how to use this book. Again, you can use all of it or very little of it. It can be read in any way you want to read it or in agreement with a professional as to what parts are relevant to your circumstances. What is more important is based on first empowering you to think about regulating your emotions and then secondly talk about emotional regulation with someone else.

Speaking to others is the one activity that, we believe, is important to accomplish, if you decide to use this book for your personal growth and change. We would recommend that whatever activities you decide to take on, that you share the results with one significant person such as, a counselor, teacher, friend or relative. The reason is that, "A book based on possibilities toward emotional regulation may only be successful in the context of making meaning out of the results." It acts as a starting point or a guideline for meaningful conversation. Over the years, I have learned that a simple accumulation of knowledge is not enough for regulating your emotions. Within knowledge is the search for wisdom, especially the wisdom found in meaningful conversation with others. For best results, pick a person you trust and talk to them about what is emotionally meaningful. The book is a catalyst for change and this becomes its true purpose in the following pages. So, do not take what is discussed in the following chapters as *the* truth, but merely as possibilities for you to explore. Please look for your own truth when attempts are made to regulate your emotions. It is hoped that such a book can help you formulate what topics or themes to discuss openly with someone who cares about you.

However, we would like to tell you about certain chapters that some people, who have used this book, found problematic. Egotism and self-hatred seem to be touchy subjects based on both appearing to cut deeply into one's attempts at self-protection. Like any other emotion in the book, there is no need to process through these emotions until you are ready. For whatever reasons, it seems these two emotions work better when revealed in groups, though that may not be your experience. Also, there are other emotions that may be problematic, including chapters on depression and apathy. Take a close look at these emotional experiences because they, at times, are confused with apathy being diagnosed as depression. It may be important to keep in mind, that people experiencing depression seem to care too much while those experiencing apathy care too little.

Another set of chapters that seem to make different statements though considered similar are, resentment and anger. Hopefully, the anger chapter will show how anger is far more impulsive than resentment; even though, people experiencing resentment are commonly sent for anger management. Another set of emotions that are grouped together but are quite different are envy and jealousy. Envy is primarily involved in an identity crisis for what people want and do not have, while jealousy is based on what people have and are insecure of losing. These may be some of the emotional experiences that you can compare, if you like.

Also, consider the emotional algorithms at the end of each chapter as generalized, step by step solutions to regulating your emotions. These algorithms, along with discussions with others, may be enough of a guide to help develop a plan for your personal regulation of emotions. However, feel free to come up with a personalized emotional algorithm based on your unique experiences. If the term emotional algorithm is unclear, you can also call them emotional maps. The term, algorithm means a step by step solution to a problem, which seems to be the case and fits the goal of this book.

Finally, these are guides to help focus your beliefs toward a more critically thought through discussion of emotions with someone else. Remember, the book acts as a guide to help empower yourself and not as a book for following someone else's expertise. Yasmeen and I hope you find meaning in regulating your emotions, and hopefully this book can help you do just that.

Peter D. Ladd
St. Lawrence University
November 30, 2017

Acknowledgements

There are a number of people we would like to acknowledge in the forming of this book. Shirley Sochia at Canton/Potsdam Hospital's Drug and Alcohol Rehabilitation Program, Potsdam NY helped enormously in the practical application of the information found in this book. Years before the idea of emotional algorithms or a holistic approach to emotions was being formed in the Mental Health Counseling Program at St. Lawrence University, Shirley was practicing this approach with clients of addiction. She is one of the major reasons this book is being published. In the past, she was kind enough to use these algorithms from pieces of paper she would give out to her clients. The success of her work with them encouraged us to seek a publisher and put these pieces of paper into print.

Anita Merrill who works at the River Hospital's Community Wellness Clinic, Alexandria Bay NY incorporated this material into their program, namely, working with combat veterans from Fort Drum, NY, and working with sexually abused clients, both in groups. She also collaborated with Yasmeen regarding a workable format for the book. River Hospital has now incorporated a few of these emotional patterns into their clinical procedures; an apathy algorithm for combat veterans and self-hatred for those who were sexually abused as children.

I (Peter) would like to thank the Native Healers on the Akwesasne Mohawk Reservation who I closely worked with in the treatment of mental health and addictions, both from a holistic perspective. They convinced me that a holistic form of psychology was compatible with traditional Native practices and ceremonies. For twenty-five years, we traded information to help those in need, who came to us for a psychological and cultural perspective. Many of the emotional patterns in this book were developed during that time and, I believe, this could not have been done without the cooperation of the Native Healers.

I (Peter) would also like to thank Kyle Blanchfield, the former President of the New York State Community Dispute Resolution Program, who systematically introduced this form of conflict resolution into State sponsored mediation and conciliation programs. The training of thousands of volunteer mediators and conciliators using these methods helped strengthen the accuracy of the emotional algorithms found in this book. It is also important to note that her dedication to conflict resolution can be seen in graduate courses that she teaches such as; Conflict Resolution, Leadership and School Violence and Leadership and School Climate.

Yasmeen and I would also like to acknowledge the input from such important graduate students who made the book far better by their input and discussions with us. Mike Elberty, Nicole Kennedy, Caroline Buskey, Clare Alai, Colleen Brethour, Christine Hanna, Paula Hance, Ashley Glover, Shirley Sochia, Anita Merrill and Aram Gomez. The level of critical thinking used by these students in discussions about the material in the book gave it an accuracy that one can only get through meaningful conversation. Also, a special thank you goes out to Sarah Zachary Grant for the time she put into editing and formatting our results.

Introduction

Emotional Regulation

Emotional regulation is defined as being able to balance between emotional rigidity and chaos/arousal. In other words, being able to keep from being overwhelmed or becoming inflexible in one's emotional responses (Siegel 2010). For example, the ability to feel fear, sadness or anger and change it to calm or peace when something traumatic has happened to you. We may have felt moments when our lives became overwhelming, and we either emotionally froze or we lost levels of control over our emotions. In your experiences, has being too rigid or chaotic had a negative impact on how you regulate personal emotions?

Emotional regulation is also about recovery time. If it takes you a few hours or a few days to recover from a highly negative emotional event, most experts would say you have a life problem, and with skills you are able to get back in life with one more moment to add to your overall life experiences. However, if it takes you weeks, months or even years to recover from a negative emotional experience, one could argue this problem has transformed itself into something that may need the help of a professional. Within this book, it is hoped that with practice you will be able to regulate your emotions more efficiently and with less stress. It may give you the ability to stay clear of or focus on disruptions as they present themselves, from both outside and inside of your experiences.

Emotional Algorithms

The next topic that may need clarification is emotional algorithms that help in regulating emotions. With practice, they can change old emotional patterns into new more emotionally regulated ones. Algorithms help people make tough decisions or any decisions. An emotional algorithm is a set of guidelines that describes how to perform a task. They are procedures or formulas for solving a problem, based on conducting a sequence of specified actions. In this book, emotional algorithms are used to help regulate personal emotions in addictions, mental health or simply those who find themselves struggling emotionally and need direction to take the next step. Here is an analogy to help you understand how an emotional algorithm works. Picture yourself on a boat and ten miles in front of you is your destination. However, to reach it you must pass through hundreds of small islands with many different channels between them. You could take your chances and try to guess your way in the direction of your destination, or buy a nautical chart book to help recognize those obstacles along the way.

In this book, we are supplying you with charts. We call them emotional algorithms based on their attempt at giving you maps or charts that may help you in regulating your emotions. They are comparable to nautical charts based on being snapshots of the actual experience you are going through. Plus, a formula for a successful journey that gets you where you want to go.

Phenomenological Research Found in this Book

Before going any further, it may be important to give you an underlying reason for reading, using and having conversations from this book. The emotional patterns in the book are based on hundreds of people describing their experiences with these emotions over the past twenty years and collecting their overall perceptions of them. So, here is the explanation for reading a book based on the experiences of others. Each of us has our unique experiences in life; however, we have in common certain phenomena or patterns that are recognizable to many different people going through these experiences. For example, each person may have their unique experiences with anger but most of us recognize a pattern of anger in ourselves and in others that is vaguely familiar. The reason we recognize anger in ourselves and others is because our minds have found a way to be orderly and efficient. Our experiences are perceived in "short hand". In other words, when we have an experience in the present, we tend to understand it by remembering a previous experience. For example, if you became angry from your experience in middle school based on finding school unreasonable, you may recognize the same pattern of anger in an unreasonable job situation later in life.

However, we do not have to specifically remember the entire previous experience but just enough of it to make the present experience, recognizable. In psychology, we might call these vaguely familiar experiences, schematic patterns or emotional maps that help us organize information as we go through life (Ladd 2012). Sometimes these schematic patterns may cause us personal conflict or possibly mental health problems, and may hinder us from other meaningful experiences. For example, being constantly jealous is a pattern of human experience that may limit our ability to socialize or to understand the world from a more intimate perspective. Though these maps tend to generalize our experiences and make them stereotypical, we continuously rely on them to understand what we are going through. Human experience is filled with vaguely recognizable patterns that may influence us both positively and negatively (Piaget 1970). The bulk of this book is in identifying and modifying negative patterns of emotion and discovering step by step emotional algorithms to change these experiences. Some people experience everyday emotions in living that are too narrow, inflexible. and possibly dangerous. By expanding these emotional patterns or adapting to new step by step emotional algorithms, people discover their freedom.

This book is dedicated to understanding negative emotional patterns and their impact on the people experiencing them. By using a phenomenological approach, our research has included specific experiences in the fields of psychology and conflict resolution. We abandoned the natural scientific method for an approach that asked the people going through these experiences to describe them and share their meaning. The results are found in research where human experience is given the highest priority and where attempts are made to clarify and rectify the damage caused by negative experiences.

Four Examples of Using Emotional Algorithms to Regulate Our Emotions

The first example is from my experience (Peter) in directing a community mental health and addictions clinic on a Native American Reservation called The Holistic Health and Wellness Program; comprised of licensed mental health counselors, certified addictions counselors and Native Healers from the tribe. This interesting combination of professionals found common ground in using these maps in all three areas as a way of pinpointing client problems from three different points of view. For twenty-five years as director of the program, I have seen the value in giving clients an opportunity to visualize their emotions especially in the areas of anxiety, depression and loss and found that other institutions have done so, as well.

The second example, resides at an inpatient drug rehabilitation program in a hospital setting where handouts of these maps were used for over ten years in presenting the emotional side of addiction. The results have pinpointed resentment, egotism and guilt as the over-riding emotional responses especially in those patients that are returning for treatment. In some respects, the emotional algorithms presented pointed to more serious problems — possibly defined as emotional addictions (Ladd 2009).

Thirdly, a Mental Health Clinic that supports a large military base is where soldiers with PTSD and other disorders can come for help. They use these emotional algorithms in their efforts to treat soldiers returning from Afghanistan and Iraq. They report that emotional patterns of apathy, loneliness and anger, are the major problems talked about in conversation with these soldiers.

Finally, I (Peter) have used these emotional algorithms in my graduate classes with teachers and counselors. It has been rewarding traveling to their classes or offices after graduating and seeing one or many of these algorithms demonstrated in drawings, pictures and handouts. It is a constant reminder of how valuable; symbols, drawings and pamphlets can be in educating others in the regulation of our emotions. Many teachers and counselors have mentioned the usefulness in showing students how they are feeling at that present moment, and then being able to help them work through these feelings. The reward has come back many times over, and I believe others have found some ownership in these emotional maps by realizing their experiences have added to the development of others.

The Importance of Meaningful Conversation in Regulating Our Emotions

For a moment, let us go back to the example of being on a boat and wanting to reach a journey's end, only hundreds of islands are in the way. The comparison was made that emotional algorithms in this book were the same as using nautical charts and how important both would be in reaching a destination. So, in using emotional algorithms to regulate your emotions, what is the destination you are seeking? We hope this book will guide you towards meaningful conversations with professionals, friends and relatives. As important as it may be to have a book that helps in finding a way through difficult emotions, it becomes experientially real when practiced in meaningful communication with others.

As one noted professional has said, "The map is not the territory." (Blanchfield 2013). Emotional algorithms may be helpful as maps, but meaningful conversations are one form of experiential territory where you grow and change. This is not only my conclusion but the conclusions of others such as; Daniel Siegel (Siegel 2016) who talks about how we reach emotional integration neurologically by having meaningful conversations with each other, or Carl Rogers (Rogers 1978) who points out the importance of positive regard, empathy and genuineness found in meaningful conversations in finding congruence and psychological healing, or Viktor Frankl (Frankl, 2000) who describes the meaning found in suffering where emotions that cause suffering, may have a purpose, if we find meaning in them. Furthermore, Frankl's statement may be the underlying premise of this journey into your emotions. So, we hope you find meaning in the book, but more importantly that you go beyond the emotional algorithm exercises and assignments, and have real-life discussions with counselors, therapists, relatives or friends. In the final analysis, meaningful conversations are at the heart of personal healing, and that especially is true when it comes to emotions.

Chapter 1: Anger

Introduction to Anger

Anger is an emotion that is built into our biological makeup, and it is connected to how we respond to life when in crisis. It is connected to a series of neuropathways in our brain, eventually leading to our crisis center called the amygdala. When we experience danger, or feel overwhelmed, anger may kick in saying to us that the present situation, has become unreasonable. This sets the amygdala into action by preparing us to either fight or flight our current situation (Ladd and Blanchfield 2016). What happens is, we experience reason not making sense when in crisis. If we already believe that much in life is unreasonable, then anger can be a constant occurrence.[1]

For some, anger might be viewed as dangerous, bad, and an undesirable outlet for what we experience as unreasonable. However, for those who understand the emotional component of the process, anger is not necessarily any of those things. It is when anger turns to violence that the negative attributes become an issue. The violent side of anger seems to define it as a rule but in everyday living there is a place for it. (Ladd and Blanchfield 2016).

It becomes important to express ourselves when life seems unreasonable. For example, in addictions and mental health counseling a meaningful expression of anger may clear the air for experiencing growth and change. Also, in everyday living, anger is not necessarily negative. It is negative expressions of it that get us in trouble. So, it may be important to keep in mind our delivery of anger. It may not be the words you are saying that gives anger a bad name. It may be your delivery of those words that shocks, startles or even makes others angry.

In the following pages take the time to immerse yourself in the emotional algorithm we are presenting. Relate to experiences that fit the steps within the algorithm. You might find that sometimes you are angry for no logical reason while other times it makes sense to express anger. Especially be aware of how you explode and do you really find closure to your anger or do you just forget about it until another unreasonable situation comes along. Being aware of our anger and how it works puts us in a more workable relationship with many of life's problems. Here is an opportunity to face an emotion that seems a bit misunderstood by those who do not give it much thought. Ultimately anger is a safety valve when reason leaves and you become stressed up and eventually explode. Take the time to understand what comes next after the explosion takes place. Hopefully this emotional algorithm of anger will either help you feel comfortable with the steps already taken with anger in your life, or give you a map to redirect it.

Emotional Pattern of Anger

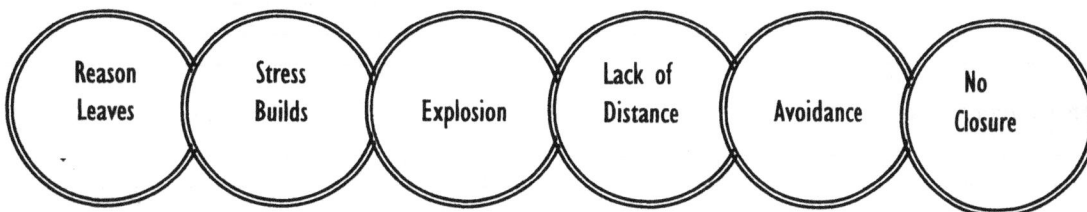

Figure 1.1

Phase 1 Reason Leaves:

All of us experience moments when life appears to be unreasonable. On these occasions, you may be ill or having a "bad-day."

Essentially situations and things that once seemed reasonable are seemingly now unreasonable. This is how a pattern of anger begins. Your reasonable thinking leaves and you prepare yourself to be angry. Typically, individuals who are having problems with anger start out with their reason leaving more frequently then they or others would like. If you find that many things in life are difficult to tolerate, or you are having trouble thinking in a reasonable way, then a pattern of anger may be disrupting your everyday experiences.

1.Describe how you handle a "bad-day"? Think of a situation and the thoughts you had at that time.

_____
_____
_____
_____

2. Whenever reason leaves do you have a similar thought pattern? What things or situations are you currently experiencing that feel unmanageable to you?

_____
_____
_____
_____

3. Think about ways in which you can help to make these experiences more manageable.

_____
_____
_____
_____

4. How can you stop the pattern of anger at this phase of the pattern? For example, identify and recognize similar thought patterns.

_____
_____
_____
_____

Phase 2 Stress Builds:

The natural and human response is to have a physical reaction when we get angry and reason has already left. We usually refer to this as "getting stressed." This is a natural physical reaction when life appears to be unreasonable. When you find life unreasonable your brain's crisis center starts to pump adrenaline through your body to prepare you for some form of an explosion. This explosion may be a physical fight with someone or a verbal screaming match. If you find that most of your surroundings are unreasonable for you, then you should be prepared to feel stressed more often than you would like.

1. On a scale from 1 – 10, with 1 being very little and 10 being very much, how much stress do you experience, daily? Describe your response.

_____
_____
_____
_____

2. How do you manage your stress?

_____
_____
_____
_____

3. What happens when you find yourself experiencing a great deal of stress?

_____
_____
_____
_____

4. How can you stop the pattern of anger at this phase of the pattern?

_____
_____
_____

Phase 3 Explosion:

If you feel as though a situation is unreasonable and your body is under stress, then an explosion of energy may soon follow. An explosion of energy may be expressed as someone yelling, physically hitting someone, or breaking something. This is what most people think of as anger. These explosions of energy are a result of your life becoming unreasonable and your body being under a great deal of stress. The type of explosion that you exhibit will determine how others treat you and/or react to you. Depending on how you express your explosion of anger may lead to your behavior being interpreted by others as unacceptable.

1. Can you think of ways you explode.

_____
_____
_____
_____

2. Do you know how others react to your explosions?

_____
_____
_____
_____

3. When you explode, do others see your behavior as unacceptable?

_____
_____
_____
_____

4. How can you stop anger at this phase of the pattern?

_____
_____
_____
_____

Phase 4 – Need for Distance:

Getting distance after an explosion may be most important in the pattern of anger. If you choose not to remove yourself from the unreasonable situation, your stress level may continue to increase which may lead to further explosions. Sometimes, the biggest problem facing individuals is that they are unable to leave a situation that feels unreasonable and has become stressful. By getting distance, you allow yourself time to cool down and bring reason back into your thought processes. Even as adults, we may need a "time-out" now and then to collect ourselves.

1. When you feel like you're about to explode, do you attempt to get away from the angering situation?

_____
_____
_____
_____

2. What are some examples of situations when you were unable to get some distance?

_____
_____
_____
_____

3. Think of some coping strategies you can use when you are in these situations.

_____
_____
_____
_____

4. How can you stop anger at this phase of the pattern?

_____
_____
_____
_____

Phase 5 Avoidance:

This is a dangerous and confusing phase in the pattern of anger. Avoidance is not a healthy form of getting distance because you are not allowing yourself time to calm down. If you avoid taking the necessary measures to calm down, then you may remain angry for a longer time. You may not be as angry as you were to start with, but this lower level of anger can stay with you most of the time. Individuals who appear to be angry most of the time have not removed themselves fully from the angering situation and fully calmed down. When they avoid their anger, they are telling their brain "I am not over being mad about this." Once you have reached this phase of the anger pattern you may become labeled an angry person.

1.Think about whether you tend to hold onto your anger or are you able to let go of it after an angry situation?

_____
_____
_____
_____

2. Do you see yourself as an angry person? Do others tend to label you as an angry person?

_____
_____
_____
_____

3. Consider some steps to take in making sure you get some distance so that you can properly calm down?

_____
_____
_____
_____

4. How can you stop the pattern of anger at this phase of the pattern?

_____
_____
_____
_____

Phase 6 Lack of Closure:

The lack of closure phase is simply explained with the statement: "At some level I still feel angry about something in my past, present, and/or future." Unfortunately, you still have a low-grade level of anger based on not working through your feelings and therefore seeing more elements in your world as unreasonable. This is how a pattern of anger seems to develop in an individual. Without bringing an end to your anger you may allow yourself to return to phase 1 and begin the pattern all over again. Now you may become locked into a pattern of anger where your angry emotions are controlling you rather than you controlling your angry emotions.

1. If any, what kinds of events or situations are you still allowing yourself to be angry about?

_____
_____
_____
_____

2. If any, why do you think you are still angry about these events or situations?

_____
_____
_____
_____

3. Think about what would help you to be able to resolve your angry feelings?

_____
_____
_____
_____

4. How can you stop the pattern of anger at this phase of the cycle so you don't begin the pattern all over again?

_____
_____
_____
_____

Exercises and Activities to Promote Healthy Emotional Responses

Problem behaviors are hard to change, even when they cause needless suffering. However, changing your behavior can begin when you start to understand why you keep doing these behaviors even when you want to stop.

1. Consider the cost and benefits of your problem behaviors:

Cost:

_____
_____
_____
_____

Benefits:

_____
_____
_____
_____

2. Think about your emotional strength:

For example, remind yourself "I am self-confident" or "I am wise" and use your strength to guide you to act differently when you feel anger.

_____
_____
_____
_____

3. It may be important to think before you act: Whenever you feel angry imagine a traffic light; red is for stop and count 1 to 10 and breathe deeply. Yellow is for thinking. Think about different things you can do and green is for go; to go and do what will be the best for you and others.
   a) Stop
   b) Think
   c) Act

4. Some people benefit from writing down five positive statements about themselves:

_____
_____
_____
_____

5. You may want to show someone you care. Think of a few kind acts people did for you when you needed them.

_____
_____
_____
_____

6. Consider self-soothing activities, for example:

   a) Mindfulness meditation
   b) Nature Walk
   c) Calming music
   d) Whatever works best

7. Poem: You may want to consider what does this poem mean to you? It could mean nothing, or it may be a place to start (Express yourself verbally or artistically; write a poem, draw a picture, write a song. Sometimes artistic expression reveals information from our unconscious that has not risen to a conscious level.) Talk about this artistic expression with someone who cares about you.

Anger
I cry out with rage with such satisfaction
Yet they tell me, it's an abnormal reaction
Maybe for them but not for me
It feels so good. How could it be?
It promptly puts fear into all my friends
Sweet explosions that must not end
It makes me a giant. It makes me a king
This civilized world, what a horrible thing
I am the beast who hunts for survival
I am the devil's newest arrival
So, look for the monster deep within
The beast in the jungle, my primitive sin

Possibilities in Therapy

Here are some of the suggestions from counselors, psychologists and psychiatrists that over the years have given input into this emotional pattern.

Phase 1 Reason Leaves:

Your therapist may want you to reflect on the dysfunctional thought process of "reason leaving" because of addictive thinking. With the help of your therapist you may want to explore how dysfunctional thoughts can create unreasonable thinking. Cognitive Behavioral Therapy may be used to develop critical thinking. In some cases, Multi-Cultural counseling is also effective if socio-cultural prejudice is causing the emotion.

Phase 2 Stress Builds:

The therapist may use different assessment tools to assess your stress levels and may also explore how your stress is affecting your biology through measuring blood pressure, heart rate etc. Physical exercise, relaxation techniques may be helpful. These techniques develop new neurological pathways and heal trauma by stimulating the brain with powerful and positive persuasion.

Phase 3 Explosion:

Be prepared to discuss your explosive behavior and different behavioral explosions that you have experienced so far. Anger management techniques may be used such as, venting with the help of Person-Centered Therapy. Your therapist may use Behavioral Therapy and ask you to explore your angry triggers.

Phase 4 Need for Distance:

The therapist may ask you to discuss the reason behind your need for distance. Be open to discuss if you are a victim of social prejudice or grew up with dysfunctional family rules. Your therapist may use Behavioral Desensitization Therapy by gradually exposing you to anger stimuli. Systems Therapy may be used to develop new social rules in your life. Some therapist use conciliation techniques to improve your relationships with others.

Phase 5 Avoidance:

The therapist may ask you to discuss your belief about avoiding anger, or explore the reason behind your avoidance of angry feelings. Cognitive Behavioral Therapy and Person-Centered Therapy may be used to expose what you are avoiding. Your therapist may recommend psychotropic medication to treat constant low levels of anger.

Phase 6 – Lack of Closure:

The therapist may explore your beliefs behind attempts at blocking closure and explore the possibility that you are addicted to your emotion of anger i.e., in the absence of such emotions you feel psychological or biological withdrawal symptoms. Your therapist may use Existential Therapy to help acknowledge your capacities and aspirations while simultaneously making peace with your limitations. Choice Therapy may also be used to improve your social relationships.

An Algorithm for Anger

Here is an emotional algorithm for anger. Again, this algorithm is a procedure or formula for solving a possible problem, based on conducting a sequence of specified actions. This is a starting point in helping you regulate your emotions. Talk about this algorithm with someone who cares about you.

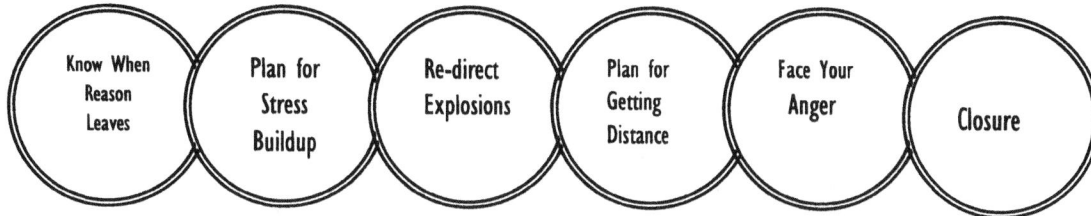

Figure 1.2

Reader's Personalized Emotional Algorithm for Anger

Now it is your turn to give direction to regulating your emotions.

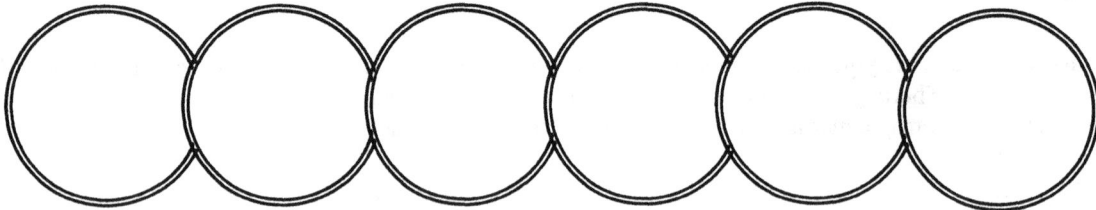

Figure 1.3

Reader's Personalized Action Plan for Emotionally Regulating Anger.

-
-
-
-
-
-

Notes

1. Powers, D. (2008). Life stress and effective well-being. *Journal of Psychology and Theology, 3*(3) 235.

Chapter 2: Anxiety

Introduction to Anxiety

Anxiety, historically has fallen into the realm of psychiatrists, psychologists, and mental health counselors. Many cases of anxiety can be recognized as mental health disorders with; General Anxiety Disorder, Post-Traumatic Stress Disorder, and Attention Deficit Disorder, just to name a few (Blanchfield and Ladd 2016). However, it is difficult to picture living in today's world without a certain amount of anxiety keeping us focused on how to face each other and our surroundings. Here is an analogy that might help us understand anxiety. Take, for example, playing a guitar. You tighten the strings at a level where the tension on them allows you to make music. If the strings are not tight enough nothing happens. If they are too tight the strings break and again no music. Anxiety is similar in that the correct balance of it helps us focus on life without under-focusing or over-focusing. Obviously, the trick is where the balance resides in any given stressful situation.[1]

As with the chapter dealing with anger, anxiety is not necessarily good or bad. It is how balanced a response you give to life's stressors and how you discover your functional or dysfunctional behavior. In some respects, it may be important to look at anxiety as inevitable. Soren Kierkegaard, the famous philosopher, said that living in this world was like walking through the raindrops of anxiety (Kierkegaard 2009). This may mean that trying to avoid anxiety is less likely to be successful than learning to face anxiety with a clear idea of how to personally treat it. We live in a world where facing anxiety becomes even more important. The uncertainty and rapid changes we experience makes facing anxiety, in some respects, a daily challenge.[2]

This chapter will help you gain a grasp on how anxiety works and how you respond to it. It also may help you realize how counter intuitive anxiety can really be. (Ladd and Churchill 2012) In other words, the more you try to stop anxiety the worse it may become. This may be why people who try to over-control their lives end up with more anxiety. The irony in this emotion is that the less you try to control it, the more in control you may be. Getting back to the guitar example, the tighter you make the strings, the less likely you fine tune the instrument. It is balancing your anxiety so that you can live a less anxious life style.

The opportunity to understand anxiety and how it relates to your life may be found in the emotional algorithm in this chapter. It will take you from the beginning stages of uncertainty through developing symptoms to how you accumulate anxiety at lower levels. This could make you more vulnerable to anxiety unless you know how to fine tune your "instrument". It also may be helpful in further collaboration with a mental health or addictions professional where the following exercises can be used as points of discussion in any ongoing counseling or therapy.

Emotional Pattern for Anxiety

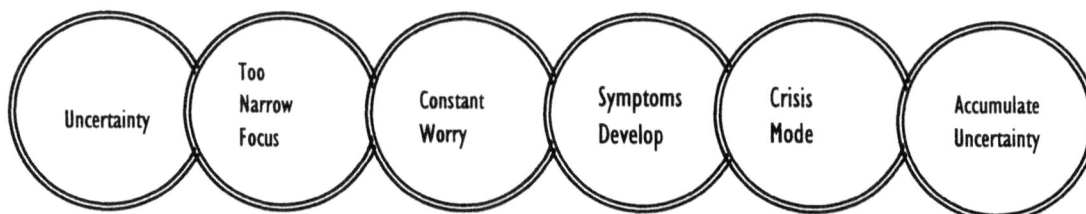

Figure 2.1

Phase 1 Uncertainty:

A pattern of anxiety starts with feeling uncertain about something in your life. At times, we all feel uncertain about things in our lives. Therefore, anxiety is a natural reaction to feeling uncertain about something that is important to you. Anxiety is different from fear. With fear, you are certain about something that is threatening such as a barking dog. If you are smart or lucky you can get away from the dog and then calm down. With anxiety, it is hard to know what to do because you are not completely clear about what exactly is threatening. Even if you are clear about the threat you may not be clear as to what you are going to do about it. In Phase 1 of anxiety, you accumulate uncertainty which may make your life more complicated and unmanageable.

1. Think about how often do you feel uncertain?

_____
_____
_____
_____

2. How do you react when you encounter situations that seem ambiguous or unclear?

_____
_____
_____
_____

3. Consider how do you cope with uncertainty?

_____
_____
_____
_____

Phase 2 Narrow Focus:

If you are experiencing uncertainty about something that is important, then usually you attempt to figure it out. For example, if someone close to you hints that he or she does not like you, then you may spend time trying to figure out why that person does not like you. You may spend a lot of time thinking about that problem. However, by spending much of your time thinking about that problem, you spend less time thinking about other important things. This narrows your thinking to those one or two problems that are causing uncertainty in your life. Here is where you can get into trouble with anxiety. It is not that you are thinking about these uncertain things, it is that you are now *not thinking* about all those other things that are important to you. You are locked into your uncertainty.

1. If you feel anxious, are you aware of your narrow focus?

_____
_____
_____
_____

2. Think about making a list of the problems you focus on the most?

_____
_____
_____
_____

3. In a day, how much time do you spend thinking about your problems?

_____
_____
_____
_____

4. If anxious, how do you cope with your narrow focus in your daily life?

_____
_____
_____
_____

Phase 3 Constant Worry:

If you are lucky or skillful, you may solve your problems and get back to thinking about many other things. If you are not so lucky then you may start to constantly worry about those uncertain situations in your life. Constantly worrying about uncertainty, wrecks many things. Here are some of them. It will be difficult to do your job or raise your family or be around your friends, and the list goes on. Constantly worrying about uncertainty in your life traps you in your own thoughts. Perhaps you may try to stop worrying about those things, but your thoughts make it difficult to stop. Most people in a pattern of anxiety bring up constant worry as one the hardest aspects of being anxious.

1. If anxious, do you narrow your focus on certain problems that eventually turn into constant worry?

_____
_____
_____
_____

2. If so, how does your constant worry affect your mental concentration when you perform your daily chores at work or at home?

_____
_____
_____
_____

3. If so, how does your constant worry affect your family, friends and colleagues?

_____
_____
_____
_____

4. If so, how does it feel when your constant worry takes up all your time and energy and makes you unable to live your life the way you would like? How do you cope with your constant worry on daily basis?

_____
_____
_____
_____

Phase 4 Symptoms Develop:

Common sense tells you that if you worry long enough and do not attend to other things in your life, then some form of physical symptoms may develop. It is your body telling you that you are worrying too much. You may start to sweat, or have an upset stomach, high blood pressure, or not be able to sleep, etc. These are the physical symptoms that most people associate with having anxiety and these are the symptoms that are treated when you take anti-anxiety or anti-depressant drugs. Sometimes these drugs relieve the symptoms and you stop worrying; other times you continue to worry though your symptoms seem less out of control. Remember that drugs treat the symptoms of anxiety, counseling may help you with the causes of it.

1. If anxious, what physical symptoms do you feel when you worry excessively?

_____
_____
_____
_____

2. Do your symptoms affect your regular daily activities?

_____
_____
_____
_____

3. What are your views about anti-anxiety drugs and do you think counseling would be helpful in your situation?

_____
_____
_____
_____

4. Are you aware of your anxious triggers? If yes, when symptoms arise how do you cope with them? List some coping strategies you use.

_____
_____
_____
_____

Phase 5 Crisis Mode:

One of the problems with a pattern of anxiety is that even when treated for it, the accumulation of constant worry and the constant battle with your symptoms may make you believe that life is a constant crisis filled with uncertainty. Believing you are going to be in crisis most of your day will continue your constant worry and reinforce your symptoms. It is easy to feel that life is one big crisis when caught in a pattern of anxiety. The constant worry and the ongoing symptoms may affect other areas of your life that you thought were not in crisis, but now they too feel like they are in crisis.

1. Do you think even a minor problem in your life can put you in crisis mode? If yes, how do you feel when that happens?

_____
_____
_____
_____

2. If anxious, how does it feel when you see other people who are also facing the same problems, but they react in a different manner?

_____
_____
_____
_____

3. If anxious, how does living constantly in crisis mode affect your energy levels?

_____
_____
_____
_____

4. Do you feel helpless and stuck when you are in crisis mode or do you think you have a strategy to come out of it? Describe a strategy you might use to come out of crisis mode.

_____
_____
_____
_____

Phase 6 Accumulate Uncertainty:

At this stage, it is easy to accumulate a great deal of anxiety because most things and situations now feel like a crisis. However, if you accumulate too much anxiety, you now are set up to experience more uncertainty. In manner of speaking, the accumulation of uncertainty can wreck your confidence or belief in yourself to get better. At this stage, the pattern of anxiety has come full circle where accumulated anxiety is creating more uncertainty. Remember, this is not accurate when people say, "I am an anxious person". He or she may feel like an anxious person or believe he/she is an anxious person. What they don't realize, they are normal people caught in a pattern of anxiety. Believing you are an anxious person, may cause more uncertainty and crisis. People experiencing anxiety feel out of control not because they really are out of control but because they *believe* they are out of control.

1. If anxious, do you think your accumulation of uncertainty is affecting your personality and beliefs? If yes, in what way?

_____
_____
_____
_____

2. Are you avoiding certain activities to protect yourself from falling into the pattern of anxiety?

_____
_____
_____
_____

3. How often do you reconsider decisions already made because you are not sure they are the right decisions?

_____
_____
_____
_____

4.With severe anxiety, how much faith do you have in the treatment process of anxiety and how willing are you to invest time and energy in this process?

_____
_____
_____
_____

Exercises and Activities to Promote Healthy Emotional Responses

Everyone experiences anxiety. This is a normal part of life, and some anxiety can even be healthy. But prolonged episodes of anxiety could be a sign of a larger problem such as an anxiety disorder.

1. List the cost and benefits of your problem behaviors:

Cost:

_____
_____
_____
_____

Benefits:

_____
_____
_____
_____

2. Getting more sleep can help reduce your anxiety: A lack of sleep will reduce the serotonin levels in your brain, which may make it harder to control your mood during the day. There are a variety of techniques that can help you get the sleep you need, but of course they only work if you are diligent at trying them, and then using the ones that work best for you.

3. Think about your emotional strengths: Many times, we dwell on the problems that we are having and forget about the emotional strengths that we have in overcoming these problems. Consider making a list of your emotional strengths. Examples like; I can love other people or I am a flexible person.

_____
_____
_____
_____

4. Think about maintaining a panic attack diary: Panic attacks will typically fade away once we lose our fear of them. But first we must understand the specifics about why they occur. In your diary, record the date, intensity level, start time and end time, symptoms, where you were when the panic attack started, what you were doing, if you were alone or with other people and what your thoughts were before the attack.

_____
_____
_____
_____

5. Deep breathing: Deep breathing is a simple technique that can be used to help with stress relief, anxiety management, mood improvement, and general well-being. It works best if you practice 10 minutes a day on a consistent basis. Find a place and time where you will not be disturbed. Make yourself comfortable in a sitting position or lie down and practice.

6. Acknowledge and recognize your anxious thoughts and feelings: By acknowledging and recognizing your anxious thoughts and feelings you may increase your awareness of the present moment while being non-judgmental. Being non-judgmental is important for taking control of your anxious thoughts and feelings. When you take control of your negative thoughts it will become easier for you to change them.

7. Poem: What does this poem mean to you? It could mean nothing, or it may be a place to start (Express yourself verbally or artistically; write a poem, draw a picture, write a song. Sometimes artistic expression reveals information from our unconscious that has not risen to a conscious level.) Talk about this artistic expression with someone who cares about you.

Anxiety
No blue horizon, no noble past
No future blueprint that will last
No redeeming colors, not even red
No chance for pleasure only dread
Caught within the face of gloom
Caught within the hands of doom
Caught outside a soothing heart
Caught again, nowhere to start
Answer this, "Will you help me?"
Will you help make me whole?
Collect those fragments, to control
Answer this, "Will you help me?"
Regain the ground that I have lost
Become myself, despite the cost

Possibilities in Therapy

Here are some of the suggestions from counselors, psychologists and psychiatrists that over the years have given input into this emotional algorithm.

Phase 1 Uncertainty:

At the beginning of your therapeutic process the therapist may assess whether you have a physical predisposition for uncertainty or have learned to depend on uncertain behavior. Your therapist may use Behavioral Therapy to treat the learned behavior of dependence or may use Bio-Counseling to make you understand the biological causes of your anxiety.

Phase 2 Narrow Focus:

The therapist may help you explore dysfunctional thinking and understand your inability to expand focus through your thoughts. The treatment may include Cognitive Behavioral Therapy to treat the obsessive-compulsive behavior.

Phase 3 Constant Worry:

Explore the cause(s) of your constant worry. Your therapist may ask you to explain your behavioral triggers while constantly worrying. The therapist may use Behavioral Therapy to treat compulsive behavior and Cognitive Behavioral Therapy to trade worries for concerns.

Phase 4 Symptoms Develop:

Your therapist may discuss the possibility of starting psychotropic drugs to control and stabilize the symptoms. Bio-Counseling may be used to explain the link between Amygdale functioning and anxiety symptoms. Physical exercise and guided imagery may also be helpful to treat anxiety symptoms.

Phase 5 Crisis Mode:

If coping with anxiety is your major approach to treatment, then medication may work for you. If you are interested in sorting out your underlying patterns of anxiety, then you may want to continue with your psychotherapy sessions and learn to change your thought patterns. Mindfulness techniques including meditation may also help to treat your anxiety symptoms.

Phase 6 Accumulate Uncertainty:

Bio-Counseling to treat constant low-grade anxiety. Person-Centered therapy and Existential Therapy may be used to understand your beliefs behind your accumulated anxiety. This process may help you to get in touch with your feelings, and understand faulty thought patterns.

An Algorithm for Anxiety

Here is an emotional algorithm for anxiety. Again, an emotional algorithm is a procedure or formula for solving a possible problem, based on conducting a sequence of specified actions. This is a starting point in helping you regulate your emotions. Talk about this algorithm with someone who cares about you.

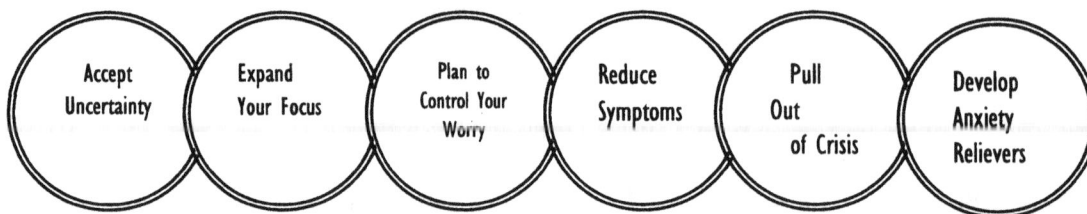

Figure 2.2

Reader's Personalized Emotional Algorithm for Anxiety

Now it is your turn to give direction to regulating your emotions.

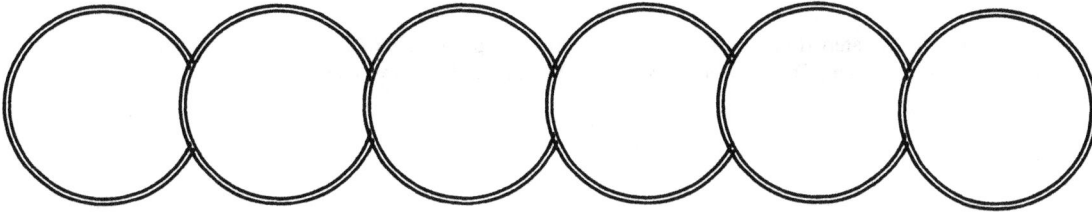

Figure 2.3

Reader's Personalized Action Plan for Emotionally Regulating Anxiety

-
-
-
-
-
-

Notes

1. Some people find it difficult to balance anxiety with living a normal life. Purkey, W. (2010). *Conflict to conciliation.* Thousand Oaks, CA: Corwin. 91–102.

2. Information about feeling threatened can be found in the following book. Blanchfield, K. E., Blanchfield, T. A.& Ladd, .P. (2008). *Conflict resolution for law enforcement: Street smart negotiating.* Flushing, NY: Looseleaf Law.17–26.

Chapter 3: Apathy

Introduction

Apathy may be considered by some as a mental disorder, or a lack of emotion by those experiencing it. Professionals may confuse apathy with depression where in depression people care too much, while in apathy they care too little; even though, people show similar behavior. For others, the experience of apathy resembles post-traumatic stress, only presenting with many small traumas as opposed to one or two large traumas. Exposure to trauma and violence through the media, your daily experiences, and chronic trauma may numb our senses and question the meaning in our lives. (Ladd 2009). Sometimes we call apathy "burn out" and that label seems to fit how people feel when their meaningful intentions turn into overwhelming stress. Under these conditions, it may seem a natural occurrence to shut down and to numb out. Well, it is! Neurologically, when we experience too much trauma we begin to shut down as a way of protection against too much trauma. Unfortunately shutting down sometimes leads to interpersonal problems where friends and relatives may criticize you for not being more involved in their lives.

Apathy is best described as a series of losses. Loss of other emotions by feeling numb, begins this downward spiral. This is followed by a loss of meaning, where not only are you feeling numb to the world, but you also do not care one way or the other. Not caring over time leads to a loss of respect in yourself and the environment around you. Ultimately, people experience a loss of hope and settle into a way of life with little positive feelings for the future.

Apathy can be a dangerous place for those looking to improve their present life. This may be why addiction and mental illness can be associated with a pattern of apathy—where some addicts become suicidal while others act out acute bouts of violence. Furthermore, apathy can be the breeding ground for depression, and other mood disorders where the environment in which you live may have a strong impact on your mental health (Ladd 2005).[1]

The emotional algorithm in this chapter may help you to not step over the line into the experience of apathy. You will see how subtly it can creep up on you where you begin losing meaning in your life, respect for yourself and looking at the world as a hopeless place. The difficulty with apathy is that it starts out as a way of protecting us from too much trauma but eventually turns into a loss of meaning, respect and hope. It is a coping mechanism that numbs you out and paints the world as a meaningless place. For example, recently we have seen numerous veterans of war experiencing post-traumatic stress from these wars. But, what happens when soldiers come home? Many can suffer from PTSD but others find their surroundings have changed and they have trouble relating not only to trauma from the past but also burn out or apathy about having a meaningful future. Whether you have experienced huge trauma in your life or have gone through a series of small traumas, apathy is an emotion that may result in major changes to what is meaningful in life.

Emotional Pattern for Apathy

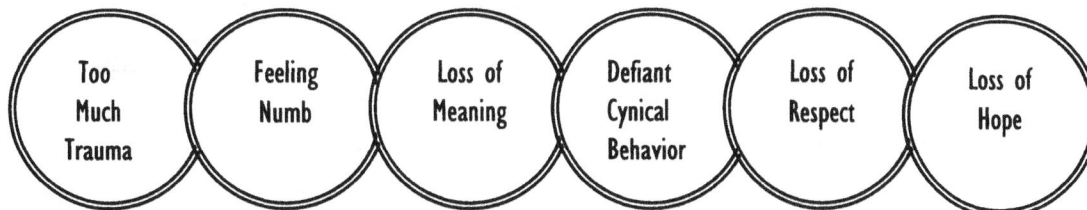

Figure: 3.1

Phase 1 —Too Much Trauma, Feeling Overwhelmed:

You may have experienced moments where life becomes stressful and you tried to cope with trauma. For example, traumatic events, trouble at work or at home, relationship problems, money problems, and so on, all can lead to accumulated trauma. At some point in your life, you may have accumulated so much trauma that you begin to feel overwhelmed. You may feel as though "Enough is enough" and you cannot cope anymore. Accumulated trauma makes these problems overwhelming. Feeling overwhelmed may not be the fault of any one thing but an accumulation of trauma that finally catches up with you. Even a strong person can feel overwhelmed.

1. Consider how difficult is it for you to get things done in a day?

_____
_____
_____
_____
_____

2. Do you have an accurate understanding of your life's problems? If so, you may want to make a list of some of these problems.

_____
_____
_____
_____

3. Think about whether life problems make you feel overwhelmed? If so, how to do you cope with your feelings?

_____
_____
_____
_____

4. How often do you feel that there is no way out of your situation?

_____
_____
_____
_____

Phase 2 Feeling Numb:

Usually, the first thing that will happen to you when feeling overwhelmed with trauma is that you have a physical reaction. Your body can only take so much. At some point, it will start to shut down those senses and could cause you to feel overwhelmed. Your body will become numb as a buffer against the trauma that has accumulated in your life. This is a normal reaction to protect you against too much trauma. However, part of the problem for someone who is becoming apathetic is that feeling numb may begin to influence areas of your life that you do not want to go numb. For example, an emergency room doctor may want a certain amount of numbness to successfully do the job. However, if the doctor goes home and is still numb, she or he may be developing a pattern of apathy.

1. Think about whether you are less concerned about your problems than you should be?

_____
_____
_____
_____

2. Do you feel less interested in having new experiences?

_____
_____
_____
_____

3. Explain how true this statement is for you. "Once a pessimistic thought pops into my head, it's like a floodgate opens - my thoughts get more and more negative."

_____
_____
_____
_____

4. Does someone have to tell you what to do each day or you just follow the same routine? If you follow the same routine, how long has it been since you have done anything new or exciting?

_____
_____
_____
_____

Phase 3 Loss of Meaning:

In a pattern of apathy, it may not take long to accept being numb as the way you normally feel. You may develop a tolerance for being numb. Unfortunately, tolerating numbness can influence meaningful things in your life that require you not to be numb — for example include loving your children or contributing to meaningful work. In other words, your physical feelings of being numb affect your beliefs. Beliefs that were important to you may seem less important. A pattern of apathy may make your meaningful projects in life seem meaningless. For example, a person experiencing a pattern of apathy may go from wanting to be a mother to not caring about being a mother, or a person who wants to help others may no longer care about helping them. Too much trauma and feeling numb have changed what was once important to a person experiencing a pattern of apathy.

1. Think about how often you feel discouraged.

_____
_____
_____
_____

2. Do you often feel that your life has no clear purpose?

_____
_____
_____
_____

3. Do you sometimes feel that you are just going through the motions in your life, as if you were running on auto-pilot?

_____
_____
_____
_____

4. Do you tend to avoid change, because adjusting to change becomes difficult? If so, please explain your concerns when you find that you cannot avoid change.

_____
_____
_____
_____

Phase 4 Defiant/Cynical Behavior:

Giving up what is meaningful to you can be a devastating experience. Many apathetic people in this position become cynical or defiant about having such meaningful beliefs in the first place. For example, a person who wanted to be successful at business may become cynical about others who are successful or someone after a divorce who wanted to be a great partner may become cynical about having a relationship with someone. Becoming cynical about what was meaningful for you may cause more apathy. You are slowly getting to the point where you do not care anymore about anything. An example of this could be people who become drug addicts or alcoholics not because they are bad people, but because of trauma and loss of meaning in life.

1. Do you have any cynical, judgmental or negative thoughts that pop into your mind when you deal with people? For example, people are untrustworthy or people always try to take advantage of me.

_____

_____

_____

_____

2. Do you feel an urge to flee when someone gets emotional around you?

_____

_____

_____

_____

3. If someone treats you unfairly or is being rude or annoying, do you tend to keep thinking about it for hours?

_____

_____

_____

_____

4. Do you find yourself getting angry in any kind of regular, predictable or cyclical pattern?

_____

_____

_____

_____

Phase 5 Loss of Respect:

Such cynical behavior in a pattern of apathy can lead to a basic loss of respect for many important things in life. It may become difficult to respect others when you do not respect yourself. This seems tragic because usually losing respect for yourself or others is not based on deciding not to care anymore. It would be more accurate to say that the pattern of apathy has worn you down to the point where too much numbness and loss of meaningful things in your life have caused you to lose respect for things that you once regarded as important, including yourself. Your thinking has turned negative based on the pattern of apathy not based on what you really want or what you really want to do. You have become burned out.

1. Do you feel useless at times? Or think you don't have much to be proud of?

_____

_____

_____

_____

2. Do you frequently or occasionally display intense dislike for others? If yes, what are the flaws in others that bother you the most?

_____

_____

_____

_____

3. Do you sometimes say to yourself "I wish that my behavior showed more respect for myself and others."?

_____

_____

_____

_____

4. A simple exercise, if you like, is to write down some "I don't care" statements.

I don't care_____
I don't care_____
I don't care_____
I don't care_____

Phase 6 Loss of Hope:

If you stay burned out long enough then you may give up hope regarding what was previously meaningful. Not feeling hopeful and not believing there is hope will affect how you look at the future. Ironically, believing there is no hope will make your life more hopeless. Not caring will attract you to other people who may not care. Without hope the possibility of feeling overwhelmed with trauma increases. By losing hope you may be setting yourself up for more traumatic experiences in life. Hopeful people seek out helpful experiences. People with little hope seek out helpless experiences.

1. Do you feel that no matter what you do, your life will stay about the same and nothing really motivates you anymore?
_____
_____
_____
_____

2. Think about whether you are losing the ability to give and receive love?
_____
_____
_____
_____

3. Please consider a list of people, activities and goals that were important to you in the past but no longer are.
_____
_____
_____
_____

4. Do you think you could once more build goal-directed behavior and develop motivation? If yes, please write the first step you could take to achieve this goal.
_____
_____
_____
_____

Exercises and Activities to Promote Healthy Emotional Responses

Problem behaviors are hard to change, even when they cause needless suffering. However, changing your behavior can begin when you start to understand why you keep repeating these behaviors even when you want to stop.

1. Think about making a list of people who can support you in various areas of your life: This exercise may help you to build your support system.
_____
_____
_____
_____

2. Words you want to hear from other people in your life: Write down a few positive words and compliments you would like to hear from people.

_____

_____

_____

_____

3. Creating Your Own Future: Create a personal mission statement. For example, what would life be like if you were able to care again?

_____

_____

_____

_____

4. Think about taking steps toward something that scares you: If you allowed yourself to do something different what would you do?

_____

_____

_____

_____

5.Think about a specific goal you have for yourself: Write down the first few steps you could take to achieve that goal.

_____

_____

_____

_____

6. Seeking Awe: Awe is the feeling of being in the presence of something vast that goes beyond our understanding of the world. Feelings of awe increase our sense of happiness and fulfillment by making us feel that we are connected to others around us. Think about making a list of experiences that give you the feelings of awe.

_____

_____

_____

_____

7. Poem: What does this poem mean to you? It could mean nothing, or it may be a place to start (Express yourself verbally or artistically; write a poem, draw a picture. Sometimes artistic expression reveals information from our unconscious that has not risen to a conscious level.) Talk about this artistic expression with someone who cares about you.

Apathy
Trying to walk and then to run
Within a place that clouds the sun.
For days and days, I try to move
To find myself. To find my groove.
But, senseless pain drains the day
Not to escape but to stay
in mangled air that sings my song.
It's just not right. It feels so wrong
Don't ask me twice to run with you
I've lost respect for what I do.
Caught within a vacant stare
I cannot feel, I just don't care

Possibilities in Therapy

Here are some of the suggestions from counselors, psychologists and psychiatrists that over the years have given input into this emotional algorithm.

Phase 1 Too Much Trauma, Feeling Overwhelmed:

The therapist could explore the cause of your overwhelming feelings and discuss your environment, life events, and daily routine, and encourage you to verbalize your feelings. Person-Centered Therapy may be used by your therapist to understand your thoughts and feelings. Narrative Therapy and Cognitive Behavioral Therapy are important to understand your apathy. The therapist may also suggest some techniques to reduce your compassion fatigue.

Phase 2 Feeling Numb:

A therapist may explain to you that feeling numb is a coping mechanism for your brain to protect itself when it is overwhelmed with trauma. Bio-Counseling may be used to understand neurological numbing. Behavioral Therapy is helpful in giving permission to take a break and take care of yourself. Debriefing Therapy would give you emotional and psychological support. Gestalt Therapy is also effective at this phase. Your therapist may ask you to role play and express your inner thoughts and feelings.

Phase 3 Loss of Meaning:

The therapist would explore your belief system to discover your negative beliefs and identify those responsible for contributing to a loss of caring about meaningful things in life. Solution Focused Therapy, Narrative Therapy; Existential Therapy may be used to bring back meaning in your life.

Phase 4 Defiant/Cynical Behavior:

The therapist might work with you to identify and challenge dysfunctional thought patterns and explore how defiant/cynical behavior can lead to antisocial behavior. Cognitive Therapy and Behavioral Therapy may be used to work with your addictive thinking. Solution-Focused-Brief Therapy may be used at this phase to treat your anti-social behavior.

Phase 5 Loss of Respect:

Your therapist might discuss with you the consequences of your loss of respect for yourself and for others, and how it is affecting your home and social environment, and making you feel alone and isolated. Suicidal Ideation Counseling along with Existential Therapy may be used by your therapist at this phase if you are feeling out on the edge. Solution Based Therapy is effective to develop social projects to find meaning and hope in your life. In some cases, Crisis Counseling may be needed to alleviate the crisis.

Phase 6 Loss of Hope:

The therapist might explore your social system which might be responsible for causing the accumulation of trauma and explore what behavior is taking place in this system. Structural System Therapy may be used if there is an emotional climate of despair. Experiential Therapy is effective when people find it hard to think about, remember, or talk about their hidden hurts.

An Algorithm for Apathy

Here is an emotional algorithm for apathy. Again, an emotional algorithm is a procedure or formula for solving a possible problem, based on conducting a sequence of specified actions. This is a starting point in helping you regulate your emotions. Talk about this algorithm with someone who cares about you.

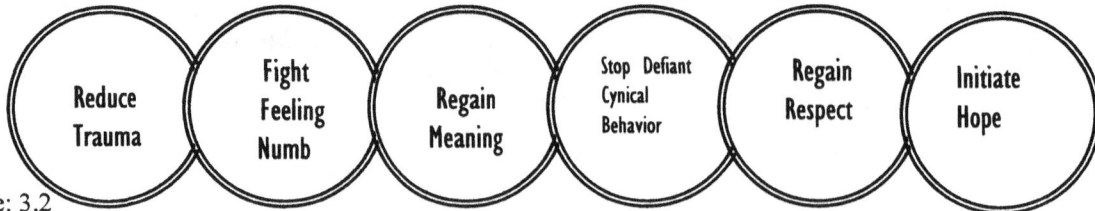

Figure: 3.2

Reader's Personalized Emotional Algorithm for Apathy

Now it is your turn to give direction in regulating your emotions

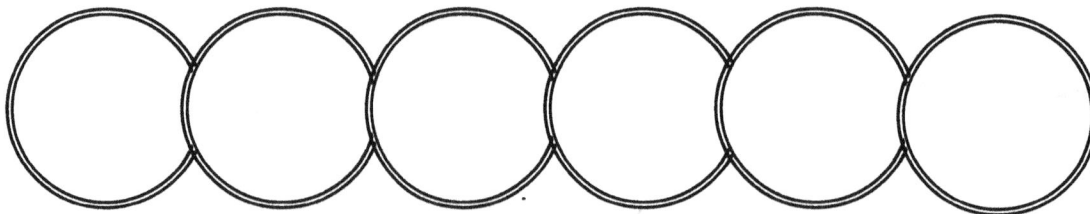

Figure: 3.3

Reader's Personalized Action Plan for Emotionally Regulating Apathy.

-
-
-
-
-
-

Notes

1. Information about creating a climate of burn out can be found in the following book. Blanchfield, K. E., & Ladd, P. D. (2013). *Leadership, violence and school climate: Case studies in creating non-violent schools.* Lanham, MD: Rowman & Little field Education. 15–39.

Chapter 4: Depression

Introduction

The idea that depression is only a biological problem does not take in the emotional side of this disorder. The experience of depression also affects a person; socially, psychologically and spiritually. The idea that the use of psychotropic drugs is all that is needed to treat depression has become a perspective by some professionals who solely adhere to a strict medical model. The reason we are including depression as one of many emotions found in this book, reflects the emotional side of depression and how emotional regulation goes beyond simply taking drugs. For example, feelings of worthlessness may become a major issue that can be best treated in a conversation with a professional, or a loved one who truly wants to help. [1]

We are not saying that treating depression should not include psychotropic drugs and for many they have been successful in regulating the emotional side of this phenomenon. However, there is a difference in finding emotional regulation and staying regulated for any length of time. In understanding an emotional pattern of depression, it may also be important in understanding how being overly sensitive is a part of emotional regulation, or how not feeling trapped may only be accomplished when others offer hope. Biologically, most of us who work in the helping professions know that a lack of interest is one of the first signs of depression, but do we know what causes this lack of interest? Is it just a shift in our biological makeup, or do life experiences affect our body and mind in such a way that the chemicals in our body begin to slow us down.

It could be that depression is a combination of interpersonal relationships affecting the neuropathways in our brains, and our neuropathways influencing how we behave around each other. To look at only one side of this experience is to overemphasize part of the depression experience, while ignoring the other side. An emotional pattern of depression found in this chapter puts an emphasis on both. As it turns out, everyday experience is a combination of things, and that is also true of depression.

The algorithm at the end of this chapter takes a more holistic approach to depression. It is a step by step guide to dealing with it. However, the plan is not simply to use psychotropic drugs and take them for an extended period, though that is the recommendation of some professionals. The algorithm in this book, denotes a more positive approach. A medical model has stated that the more episodes of depression you experience, the more severe they may become. We have the opposite belief. If you have a road map for dealing with depression, future episodes may become weaker while you become more resilient. Here is your chance to come up with your personal conclusions regarding depression and think carefully about if or when it enters your life.

Emotional Pattern of Depression

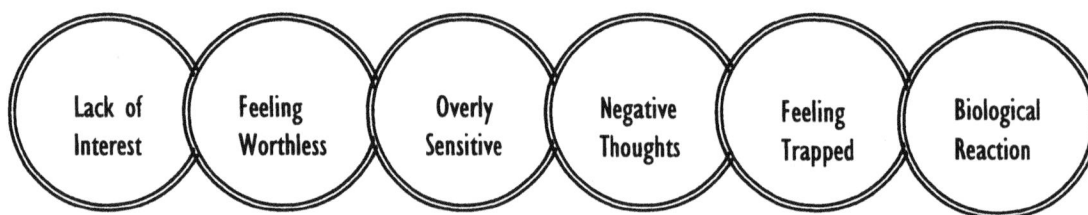

Figure: 4.1

Phase 1 Lack of Interest:

The controversy with depression continues. Is the lack of interest in life activities causing a biological reaction and making one depressed or is the biological reaction causing the lack of interest? The depression may start from one of these starting points. To understand depression, it would be helpful to explore and find the moment when you lost interest in your life experiences. During that time, you may have experienced less enjoyment in things that were important and pleasurable to you. There could be a physical reaction as well. You may notice that around that time you may have lost appetite or began eating more than usual or noticed changes in your sleeping patterns. You may find it difficult to sleep or you sleep more than usual or in some cases, you may find it difficult returning to sleep once you are up in the middle of the night. These sleep changes may also mean that your depression is being combined with anxiety which keeps you awake.

1. Do you often get bored with your life?

_____
_____
_____
_____

2. What energized your interest in the past?

_____
_____
_____
_____

3. Do you prefer to stay home rather than going out and doing new things? If so, when was the last time you pursued a new interest?

_____
_____
_____
_____

4. Do you feel satisfied with your life? If not, please explain briefly the reason(s).

_____
_____
_____
_____

Phase 2 Feeling Worthless:

Experiencing lack of interest affects the way you see yourself. Overtime, you may feel out of sync with everyone else and begin to feel worthless. If once you were an interesting and outgoing person and you have taken quite a jolt from being an interesting person to lacking interest in activities you had enjoyed in the past, then a pattern of depression may be taking hold. Therefore, it would become easier for you to convince yourself that you are doing something wrong. At this phase, some people develop intense feelings of guilt for not having interest anymore and start feeling worthless. Realistically, your depression is partially about experiencing loss; loss of interest, loss of appetite, loss of pleasure, loss of sleep, etc. It is not difficult to understand why you would feel worthless under these conditions. The feelings and the negative thought patterns at this phase make it easier to feel like a failure.

1. How often do you feel that you don't have what it takes to succeed in life? If often, what qualities do you wish you had to be successful?

_____
_____
_____
_____

2. Do you become self-critical when things don't come out just right? If so, write down some of the labels you put on yourself.

_____
_____
_____
_____

3. Do you think that most people are better off than you are?

_____
_____
_____
_____

4. Do you often feel crushed by a sense of worthlessness? If so, write down the ways you cope with the feeling.

_____
_____
_____
_____

Phase 3 Overly Sensitive:

If your lack of interest and feeling worthless have accomplished anything at this point, it is that you have become overly sensitive to just about everything. Many times, you will find simple things in life that you handled easily, as impossible to do. Life seems exaggerated only in a negative way. If you cannot do these everyday things then what can you do? Instead of believing that it will pass, you critically pass judgment on yourself and become extremely hard on yourself. Maybe this is the moment to be fair with yourself. You did not decide to stop being interested in life neither did you plan to feel worthless. Maybe all of these disruptions in your life have made you an obsessive negative thinker. Maybe your over sensitivity is because you want to feel better and you don't know how. Therefore, you feel exhausted at times when you try too hard to look normal.

1. How much do other people's negative moods affect your thoughts and feelings?

_____
_____
_____
_____

2. Do you often worry about hurting other people's feelings?

_____
_____
_____
_____

3. If a friend doesn't return your call or text, do you often assume he or she is angry with you? If so, please write an example when your negative thoughts turn out to be unrealistic?

_____
_____
_____
_____

4. Do you tend to ruminate on negative information and things that occur in your life? If so, write a few things you ruminate about.

_____
_____
_____
_____

Phase 4 Negative Thoughts:

Trying too hard can cause problems in your thinking. When you try to solve a problem but cannot solve it, then you might wear yourself down by trying too hard. Here is where anxiety and depression start to work together. Constantly trying to get out of your depression and being unsuccessful at it, will cause anxiety to creep into the process. Unfortunately, anxiety will not help someone who is feeling worthless and has become overly sensitive to life. It may make you become obsessed with trying to get out of your depression, where the harder you try the worse you feel. Furthermore, these obsessive thoughts are not positive thoughts but negative ones. Constantly thinking negative thoughts about something that means so much to you but seems unobtainable can eventually wear down your confidence. It is not too difficult to convince yourself that you will stay depressed for a long time.

1. Do you often worry that you won't be able to carry through your intentions? If so, what are the most pressing negative thoughts that come to your mind?

_____
_____
_____
_____
_____

2. What negative thoughts go through your mind when you are confronted with change or start something new in your life?

_____
_____
_____
_____
_____

3. Do you often start out expecting the worst, even though sometimes you know you will probably do just fine? If so, please write an example where you were expecting the worse but things turned out quite the opposite.

_____
_____
_____
_____
_____

4. How do you feel when you don't measure up to others' expectations?

_____
_____
_____
_____
_____

Phase 5 Feeling Trapped:

At this phase, you feel trapped in your depression. The pattern of depression has made you feel that way; not that you normally feel trapped in your life. This is important, because if you think you are a trapped person, then you may give up hope and have hopeless thoughts. It is probably better to believe that the pattern of depression has trapped you and once you are out of this pattern, you will be yourself again. Here is where your belief about yourself becomes important. It is better to believe you are trapped in a pattern than believing you have developed depression as a part of your identity. Labels such as "I am a depressed person" will only trap you more. You may begin to believe that your worthlessness and over sensitivity and negative thoughts are about who you are, rather than the pattern you are in.

1. Do you often feel helpless? If so, what are some of the things in your life that triggered the most overwhelming feeling of helplessness?

_____
_____
_____
_____

2. What do you currently do that drains you?

_____
_____
_____
_____

3. What are the events, situations, or thoughts that trigger some level of self-doubt?

_____
_____
_____
_____

4. Have you ever thought of self-harm? If so, how many times and what triggered the urge to self-harm?

_____

_____

_____

_____

Phase 6 Biological Reaction:

If you think believing you *are* a depressed person is not going to have an impact on your body, then think again. Our beliefs have an enormous influence on our brain circuitry. As stated in phase one, it is hard to determine which came first "The chicken or the egg." Yet does it matter whether you lose interest and that affects your mind's circuits? First, there are anti-anxiety drugs and anti-depression drugs that may help reinforce your brain's circuits and help you deal with the symptoms of depression. However, these drugs may help you feel better but they become less effective in keeping you better. You may want to talk to a mental health counselor about those experiences in your life that caused you; to lose interest or those experiences where you felt worthless. You also may want to explore when you were overly sensitive in your life and how you handled feeling that way. You may want to explore those moments when you seem to develop negative thinking or what situations in life made you feel trapped. In this way, you will not only be dealing with the symptoms of depression. You will be dealing with the pattern of depression that explains your unique experience with it.

1. Do you suffer from unexplained aches and pains (such as headache, stomach pain, joint pain or other pains?) If so, please describe below.

_____

_____

_____

_____

2. Are you having difficulty falling asleep or staying asleep or are you sleeping too much?

_____

_____

_____

_____

3. Do you often feel fatigued, sluggish, and physically drained and have trouble focusing, making decisions, or remembering things.

_____

_____

_____

_____

4. Are you experiencing increased or reduced appetite? If so, please write down your daily meal timings and food intake.

_____

_____

_____

_____

Exercises and Activities to Promote Healthy Emotional Response

People caught in a pattern of depression feel disconnected, lost, and confused, and everything around them looks and may feel dark and bleak. Even though they have no reason to feel this way, it feels all too real for them. These exercises and activities can be used to help people understand how pessimistic thinking is affecting their mental health.

1.Break the Cycle of Stress and Depression: There is a connection between stress and depression. Dealing with stress in a constructive way can be an important part of overcoming depression. The following exercises show you things you can do every day to fight the impact of stress on your depression.

    1.Scheduled Relaxation Activities: For example, deep breathing, meditation, relax with quiet music etc.
    2.Self-Care: 7-9 hours of sleep, good nutrition, physical exercise etc.
    3.Time Management: Such as making realistic goals and steps to achieve them and realistic scheduling and planning.
    4.Creative Fun Activities
    5.Any other activities you can do to reduce stress.

2. Positive Emotions: Whenever you feel down, thinking about things that trigger positive emotions can help. For example:

    1.Think about one thing that always brings you joy.
    2.Think about something that always makes you hopeful
    3.Think about a person who always makes you feel love.
    4.Think about the moment when you really felt proud of yourself.

3. Daily Gratitude: This exercise would help you to turn thoughts outward and feel grateful every day. At the end of each day, write down three things you are grateful for. It could be anything. For example, a smile from a stranger, a call from a friend, a morning walk, finding a new recipe, a compliment at work, whatever brightened your day. Write three things you are grateful for right now:

_____
_____
_____
_____

4. Write down five positive statements about yourself:

_____
_____
_____
_____
_____

5. Become aware of your emotional strength:
For example, when you feel depressed remind yourself "I am self-confident" or "I am worthy" and use your strength to control your negative emotion.

_____
_____
_____
_____

6. Seeking Awe: Awe is the feeling of being in the presence of something vast that transcends our understanding of the world. Feelings of awe increase our sense of happiness and fulfillment by making us feel that we are connected to others around us. Make a list of experiences that give you feelings of awe.

_____
_____
_____
_____

7.What does this poem mean to you? It could mean nothing, or it may be a place to start (Express yourself verbally or artistically write a poem, draw a picture, write a song. Sometimes artistic expression reveals information from our unconscious that has not risen to a conscious level.) Talk about this artistic expression with someone who cares about you.

Depression

Distant Shades of Calm
A Capsized Smile
Frozen Patchwork Stare
Gripping to Crumbling Air
A Pencil Line of Teardrop
Clinging to a Desert You
Waiting for a Moment to
Sail the Barren Cheek
Neither strong nor weak
A prelude ramble,
before you speak

Possibilities in Therapy

Here are some of the suggestions from counselors, psychologists and psychiatrists that over the years have given input into this emotional algorithm.

Phase 1 Lack of Interest:

A therapist may explore your life experiences that are causing loss of interest. Your lack of interest may be generated by a pattern of negative thinking practiced by you over time. Person-Centered Therapy is an effective treatment for the negative thinking associated with lacking interest. Your therapist may discuss the use of SSRI's to balance the neurotransmitters in the brain which would helpful in generating a positive response to feeling lack of pleasure.

Phase 2 Feeling Worthless:

A therapist may ask you the meaning behind feeling worthless and explore if that feeling is based on an overemphasis on dysfunctional thinking and other such problems. Some form of Existential Therapy may be helpful in finding the reasons behind your feeling of worthlessness. Schema Therapy is helpful if the feeling is generated from traumatic and negative childhood experiences.

Phase 3 Overly Sensitive:

A therapist may discuss your emotional experiences that are causing oversensitivity and may explore what thoughts go into being overly sensitive. A therapist may discuss how your oversensitivity is effecting you and your social life. Your therapist may discuss the option of using psychotropic drugs because in some cases these drugs can help reduce the experience of oversensitivity, especially when anxiety is associated with the experience. If you find it difficult to control your emotions, your therapist may use Emotion-Focused Therapy. This therapy would help you to recognize and control your visceral emotions.

Phase 4 Negative Thoughts:

A therapist may discuss with you how obsessive negative thinking may lead to anxiety and explore your failed attempts at recovery and how these failures contribute to obsessive thinking and behavior. A therapist may suggest some form of spiritual treatment, such as the use of meditation or other relaxation techniques, to stop the flow of obsessive thoughts and feelings. In some cases, Solution-Based Therapy is helpful to create hope because this therapy builds on a person's strengths and brings into focus alternative solutions that will create hope.

Phase 5 Feeling Trapped:

A therapist may explore your beliefs and meaning behind your feeling trapped. Capturing the essence of feeling trapped may make the diagnosis more personal and help to strengthen the therapeutic alliance between you and your therapist. With the help of your therapist, mapping out how you arrived at a defeatist attitude, what such attitude means to you, and how such an attitude working in your life may help you to understand your thought patterns and motivate you to change. Your therapist may discuss the severity of your feeling trapped especially if you are having suicidal ideation. Depending upon the severity of the feeling some form of Cognitive Behavioral Therapy may be helpful.

Phase 6 Biological Reaction:

Cognitive Behavioral Therapy (CBT) is often the treatment of choice if you are experiencing a biological reaction to your depression. This therapy helps people learn ways to cope with and solve their problems as they gain a deeper understanding of their condition or circumstances. You will also learn to set realistic life goals and identify and change behaviors or thoughts that have negative effects on your life.

An Emotional Algorithm for Depression

Here is an emotional algorithm for Depression. Again, an emotional algorithm is a procedure or formula for solving a possible problem, based on conducting a sequence of specified actions. This is a starting point in helping you regulate your emotions. Talk about this algorithm with someone who cares about you.

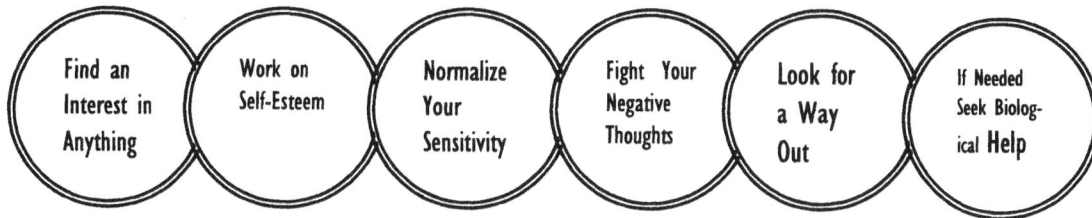

Figure 4.2

Reader's Personalized Emotional Algorithm for Depression

Now it is your turn to give direction to regulating your emotion

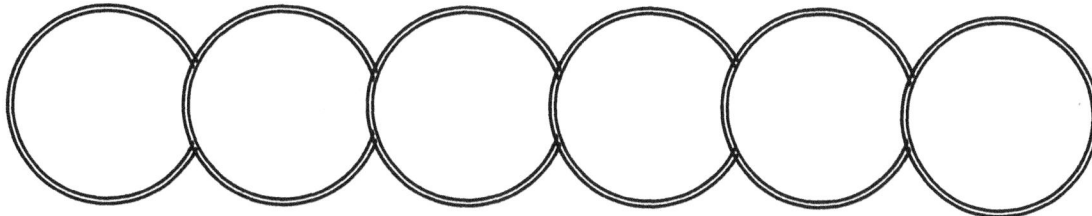

Figure 4.3

Reader's Personalized Action Plan for Emotionally Regulating Depression.

-
-
-
-
-
-

Notes

1. Having worthless feelings can be found in the book Ladd, P. & Churchill, A. (2012) London, UK: Jessica Kingsley Pub.

Chapter 5: Egotism

Introduction to Egotism

Egotism can be identified as insecurity being masked with confidence (Ladd 2009). On occasions this takes place in a competitive environment where the perception of confidence may be as important as actual feelings of confidence. A person may believe that, "putting your guard down" may signal weakness or vulnerability. Here we see someone who tries to take over any given relationship by using some form of force. Maybe you have met that person who is constantly telling you that "you are wrong" and "he or she is right." Or, maybe you find yourself acting that way because you truly believe you are right most of the time. Unfortunately, with this emotion you can be right and wrong at the same time. What you say may be correct, but your delivery may talk down to others where they find it difficult to listen to you.

Take for example, friends or relatives who believe their opinions should be accepted and their way of life should be your way of living. They may tell you how your decisions are the wrong ones and if you would only listen to them, things would go better for you. Are they really trying to help you or are they bragging about themselves? When your ego gets in the way of wanting to help someone, it becomes difficult for the other party to know the difference.

Consider this other point when feeling egotistical. Insecure people may need to be the center of attention as a way of controlling other's feelings about them. Egotistical people may have a similar need. They may need to be right as their way of holding on to control. However, both of these examples are based on a level of insecurity that needs to be covered up with a sense of false confidence.

For better or worse, we do seem to put up with much of the behavior found in experiencing egotistical people. Our families, workplaces and communities may sadly allow these people to practice egotism by saying they are right, and if we do not stop them, they will wrongly believe they earned that right by just saying it. Feeling secure may take more than saying you are right to actually be right. It may require suffering through the pain of one's convictions to earn such a right. In some respects, egotism tries to make things right even though they may not be accurate. For some, egotism may, at times, border on lying about the facts in any given situation. A person's need to be right becomes more important than the truth.

The following chapter may describe someone you know that acts in an egotistical manner, or it may describe yourself. Try using the chapter either way. However, here is a point to remember. If you are practicing egotism, you may not want to admit it. Your need to be right may be stronger than your need to admit you are an egotist. Nevertheless, the chapter can be beneficial either way as far as emotional regulation of a phenomenon that we quite often witness in life. For those of you who live, work and are engaged as an egotist or encounter one, the chapter may help you understand what is taking place.

Emotional Pattern for Egotism

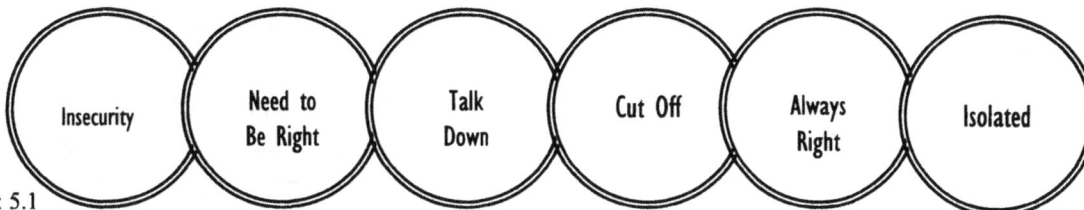

Figure: 5.1

Phase 1 Insecurity:

This pattern may be difficult for any of us to admit but the truth is that, at times we all have feelings of insecurity, while acting otherwise. First, nobody expects you to be secure all the time and second, nobody expects you to act insecure around others. All of us will act this way occasionally. However, when you feel insecure but are hiding it from others by acting in ways where it seems; nothing bothers you or you know more than anyone else or you want to impress others with your security, then a pattern of egotism may develop. For whatever reason, you may need to put up a false front to hide your insecurity while tricking yourself into believing you really are secure.

1. Do you get easily annoyed by people who do not treat you with as much respect and adoration as you feel that you deserve?

_____
_____
_____
_____

2. How often do you feel that you need to reject people before they reject you?

_____
_____
_____
_____

3. When you go to a party or to any social gathering do you or someone else usually like to have a "grand entrance" so that everyone notices?

_____
_____
_____
_____

4. Do you feel at your best when people seek you out and ask for advice on all issues of their lives?

_____
_____
_____
_____

Phase 2 Need to Be Right:

One of the most common ways you can trick yourself into believing that you are secure when you are not, is by making sure that you act like you are right most of the time. The more you can convince yourself that your position is right, the more you inaccurately believe you are safe and secure. By the way, when your position is right, but you are open to other points of view, you can add to your self-esteem and confidence. So, most of us *want to be right*, when we take a stand and defend; thoughts, feelings, or behavior. However, in a pattern of egotism, it is not that you want to be right. You *need to be right*. That means you must make sure you are always right, but by doing this, it also ensures that everyone must always be wrong. Herein lies the inaccuracy found in a pattern of egotism. If you need to be right most of the time, you will become more insecure because no one can be right that much of the time.

1. Is it difficult for you to doubt your view of things? If so, how do you feel when someone tries to convince you that your view is not the right one?

_____
_____
_____
_____

2. When in an argument, is it difficult for you to concede? Think of an example and describe how you felt at that moment?

_____
_____
_____
_____

3. How often do you feel it is your duty to influence other people's decisions or lifestyle choices? If you often feel that way, think of an example when you tried to intervene and someone took offense.

_____
_____
_____
_____

4. What are your concerns if you are proved to be wrong?

_____
_____
_____
_____

Phase 3 Talk Down to Others:

The belief that "I need to be right" sets the stage for some self-righteous and condescending behavior in a pattern of egotism. You may start talking down to others to defend your need to be right. Even when you know your point of view is wrong, you may still talk down to others. Again, another faulty belief is behind being self-righteous and talking down to others namely, "If I talk down to others, then I will control the situation, and if I control the situation, then I will feel more secure and of course, be right." Unfortunately, getting caught in this pattern may blind you to how others are seeing you. They may instead see you as a bully or braggart or an obnoxious person, and they may even begin talking about you behind your back.

1. When you review someone else's performance, do you find something wrong most of the time?

_____
_____
_____
_____

2. When someone corrects you, what is your initial reaction? Do you become defensive?

_____
_____
_____
_____

3. Do you usually find it more efficient to handle something yourself than to explain to others how it ought to be done?

_____
_____
_____
_____

4. How often do you believe your views are the truth, and your conclusions must be accepted by other people? What kind of reaction do you get from people when you try to tell them your "truth".

_____
_____
_____
_____

Phase 4 Cut Off from Others:

Besides the possibilities of talking behind your back, people may find other ways of avoiding you. Very few people want to be around someone who talks down to others, except possibly others who talk down to people. However, in a pattern of egotism being right and talking down to others seems more important than connecting with others. So, not being part of the group may not be something that you seek out or value; even though, you may feel outside the circle. You may be alone but you probably have not exposed your insecurity.

1. Please write some of the incorrect views people have about you.

_____
_____
_____
_____

2. If you lose an argument to someone, do you feel deep inner rage towards that person?

_____
_____
_____
_____

3. Do you often feel as if no one understands you?

_____
_____
_____
_____

4. Do you sometimes feel that it would be better to be alone than arguing and explaining your point of view to other people?

_____
_____
_____
_____

Phase 5 Defend Your Position at All Costs:

In some ways as you go through this pattern, the chances of you feeling more insecure increases while your behavior may become more inflexible. Many people caught in this pattern will defend their point of view at all costs, even if it makes others dislike them even more. When you look at this type of defense, it does not make much sense. By defending your position at all costs, you can become more insecure while others now can view you as even more inflexible. The belief that defending your position at all costs will make you more secure, does not seem to hold true. Ironically, it may cause insecurity and continue to cut you off from others.

1. Do you view criticism as unnecessarily harsh?

_____
_____
_____
_____

2. If you have offended someone in the past, is it difficult for you to understand why they took it so badly?

_____
_____
_____
_____

3. Think of an example when you thought you were right and you defended your point of view but as a result you lost a relationship, or an opportunity or a job.

_____
_____
_____
_____

4. If you had lost something significant in the past because of your inflexible behavior and you get a chance to go back in time and fix it, how would you do it differently?

_____
_____
_____
_____

Phase 6 Isolation:

Ultimately, you may feel isolated from others with no increase in security. The belief that you "needed to be right" may cause you loneliness or at least feelings of isolation. Again, how can this help with your security? It probably will make things worse. Instead, it may make you more insecure while convincing yourself that the only way to solve your problem is to go through the pattern once again. This is how people end up losing friends and becoming unpopular, yet continue to practice the pattern that made them that way. Unfortunately, one of the biggest problems with this pattern is denial. When someone looks at this pattern who practices it in real life, usually they say, "That is not me or I am not insecure."

1. Think about how many close dependable friends do you have and how often do you see them?

_____
_____
_____
_____

2. Consider when you are going through difficulty who do you talk to or ask for advice?

_____
_____
_____
_____

3. Do you sometimes feel as if no one understands you?

_____
_____
_____
_____

4. Do you sometimes feel excluded from your social circle or does it seem like your friends are closer among themselves than with you?

_____
_____
_____
_____

Exercises and Activities to Promote Healthy Emotional Responses

Emotional intelligence begins with learning to recognize your emotions and the effect your emotions have on your behavior. This is especially true with egotism.

1. List the cost and benefits of your behaviors:

Cost:

_____
_____

Benefits:

_____
_____

2. Make a list of five people who have positive feelings towards you.

_____
_____
_____
_____

3. The next time you have a disagreement with someone, think about how you acted by filling out the following questions:

    a)   The disagreement was about? _____
    b)   Did you stick to the topic? _____
    c)   How long did the disagreement last? _____
    d)   Did you treat the person with respect? _____
    e)   Were you listening carefully to the other person? _____
    f)   Did you bring up compromises or solutions to the problem? _____

4. Think before you act: Whenever you are in argument imagine a traffic light. Red is for stop. Yellow is for thinking. Think about respectful ways to convey your point of view. Green is for saying what will be the best for you and others.

   a) Stop
   b) Think
   c) Act

5. Practice humility:

   a) In a conversation, focus intently on what the other person is saying and not on what you will say next.
   b) Practice active listening and talk less.
   c) Prefer someone's needs over yours.
   d) When someone says something that does not agree with your opinion, consider holding your tongue and letting it go.

6. Build a support system and find people with common interest. Being connected to others is an important part of your mental health and happiness. If you are isolated and want to make more social connections, you will usually have more success when you participate in groups of people with common interests.

7. What does this poem mean to you? It could mean nothing, or it may be a place to start (Express yourself verbally or artistically; write a poem, draw a picture, write a song. Sometimes artistic expression reveals information from our unconscious that has not risen to a conscious level.) Talk about this artistic expression with someone who cares about you.

Egotism

Instantaneous handshake man
Who smiles before he never can
No longer be
Apart of nature's timeless me
Or you
Who takes a stand

Possibilities in Therapy

Here are some of the suggestions from counsellors, psychologists and psychiatrists that over the years have given input into this emotional algorithm.

Phase 1 Insecurity:

A therapist might ask you to discuss your upbringing and belief system in depth. Existential Therapy may be used to expose your flaws in your belief system. Rational Emotive Therapy is useful to understand the illusion of control. Person-Centered Therapy is effective for developing a strong therapeutic relationship.

Phase 2 Need to Be Right:

A therapist might explore your beliefs and thoughts and point out what thoughts and beliefs are behind your need to be right most of the time. Behavioral Therapy would be effective to treat your control issues and Existential Therapy would help you reflect on your belief system.

Phase 3 Talk Down to Others:

A therapist may ask you to discuss the way you convey your point of view and your behavior with people in general. How do you treat your colleagues, subordinates and your superiors as well as your friends and family? Your therapist may work on developing your communication skills. Behavioral Therapy is effective in making positive changes in your behavior and learning to manage your stress. Your therapist may help you to identify your compulsive triggers.

Phase 4 Cut Off from Others:

Your therapist may point out the thought process that allows you to be cut off from others and might explore the reason behind your rigid social boundaries. Structural System Therapy may be used to build and identify boundaries. Cognitive Behavioral Therapy and Solution Focused therapy is an effective treatment at this phase.

Phase 5 Defend Your Position at All Costs:

A therapist may further discuss your beliefs behind defending your position at any cost while denying other person's point of view. Cognitive Behavioral Therapy may be helpful to develop critical thinking. Psychoanalysis may expose your defense mechanism. Existential Therapy may be used by your therapist to expose your inflexible belief system.

Phase 6 Isolation:

Your therapist may use Existential Therapy to discuss; your upbringing, life events, belief system, and thought process. This may help in pointing out the factors which contributed to your isolation. Family Therapy may be used to improve your relationship skills. Person-Centered Therapy is beneficial when you develop a positive and strong therapeutic alliance with your therapist.

An Emotional Algorithm for Egotism

Here is an emotional algorithm for anxiety. Again, an emotional algorithm is a procedure or formula for solving a possible problem, based on conducting a sequence of specified actions. This is a starting point in helping you regulate your emotions. Talk about this algorithm with someone who cares about you.

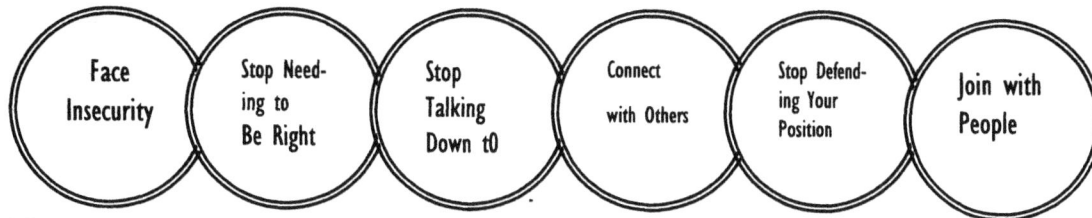

Figure 5.2

Reader's Personalized Emotional Map for Egotism

Now it is your turn to give direction to regulating your emotions

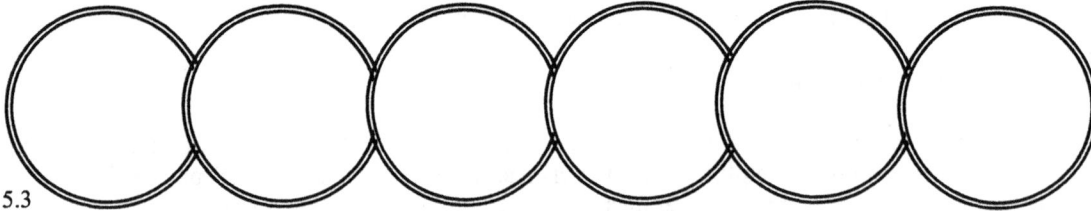

Figure 5.3

Reader's Personalized Action Plan for Emotionally Regulating Egotism

-
-
-
-
-
-

Chapter 6: Envy

Introduction

We live in a society of celebrities, heroes and icons. As we develop, the influence of these people has a tremendous impact on our identity. This reality makes its way into how we see ourselves, especially in adolescence. This is a time where someone is outgrowing childhood and still has not reached the stature of an adult. So, it seems perfectly acceptable in trying to emulate someone else who you admire. Take for example any rock star. You are sixteen looking to fit in with others and the mood, behavior and "look" of this successful "rocker" changes the way you act around others. To some, such an experience can be viewed as the rock star acting as a role model for who you would like to be as an adult. This common developmental experience may help guide you toward adulthood until facets of your personal identity take hold and fill out the rest of who you would like to be.[1]

On the other hand, your wanting to be someone else may be the person down the street who appears more popular, intelligent and attractive. It may be, you do not necessarily use this person as a role model but try to be exactly like them even though for all practical purposes, you never will be them. This may lead you into an identity crisis where instead of working on your personal identity, there is this constant comparing yourself with others. Furthermore, since you cannot be other people, there may develop this love/hate relationship with those you emulate.

Take for example someone who believes being acceptable will only happen if he or she loses weight. This person might strive so hard to be acceptable that what happens is identified as an eating disorder. At the base of this example is someone who envies the identity of thin people with not giving much of a chance to the development of those great characteristics found in one's self. In this chapter, you have the opportunity to sort this out. The algorithm presented was primarily made up from people who admitted to having an identity crisis where envy was at the root of their problem. Good luck in finding those characteristics that define your identity.

Emotional Pattern for Envy

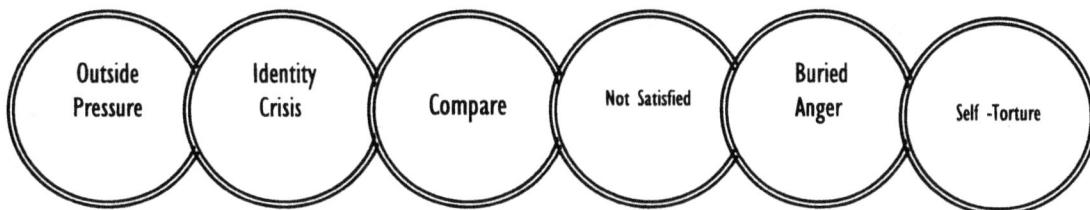

Figure 6.1

Phase 1 Outside Pressure:

Envy may be difficult to avoid in a society where achievement and looking a certain way is associated with being an acceptable or unacceptable person. For example, for some, the social pressure of being thin, rich, or popular may make you believe that you need to live up to these standards. A female teenager may believe that she needs to lose weight to be acceptable to her friends and family, or a young adult may believe that social pressures from society will be their guide to happiness. All of us are influenced by outside social pressures, for example, top students want to get the highest grade or a flashy dresser wants the latest style of clothing. These are the thought patterns of some of us who believe it is important to conform with social pressure to feel content and happy.

1. Consider how perfect do you think your life is according to societal and cultural standards?

_____
_____
_____
_____

2. Consider making a hierarchy of your life goals and standards you wish to achieve.

_____
_____
_____
_____

3. How often do you think that life is not giving you exactly what you need to grow and be happy?

_____
_____
_____
_____

4. How important to you is being well-liked and physically attractive?

_____
_____
_____
_____

Phase 2 Identity Crisis:

A thought pattern of envy begins when giving into outside pressures become the biggest part of your identity. In other words, outside pressure controls how you see yourself or what you believe is important, not what you have figured out is important for yourself. People who base their identity solely on outside pressures may have an identity crisis when that outside pressure changes. For example, if society says that I should be thin and I become thin and then society changes its mind and says that I should be muscular, then I better get working on being muscular. The point to make is that now you are in a pattern of not taking control of your personal identity but waiting for outside pressures to define it. If nothing else, this may create anxiety by giving your center of control *over* to someone or something outside of you. You may find it difficult in this pattern to find a personal identity that allows you to feel in control of your own life.

1. Do you repeatedly ask yourself: Who am I? What am I doing? What do I want? If so, what aspects of your life and your identity confuse you the most?

_____
_____
_____
_____

2. Is your life not turning out like you planned?

_____
_____
_____
_____

3. Do you sometimes have a sudden, intense fear of failure?

_____
_____
_____
_____

4. When you think of the future, are you sometimes filled with feelings of panic?

_____
_____
_____
_____

Phase 3 Compare:

Instead of figuring out what makes up your identity, you may begin comparing yourself to others who fit the outside image that you find desirable. In a pattern of envy, this can be a trap because it makes your identity important or valuable only if you compare favorably to someone else. For example, someone who constantly loses weight may not feel good about his/herself if the person he or she is trying to look like turns out to be thinner. The behavior that is most noticeable in a pattern of envy is the experience of constant comparison. In a pattern of envy, you may have a problem with stopping the comparisons when you have bought into the outside pressures controlling your identity. Outside pressures may encourage you to continue to compare.

1. When you look at people your age, how do you feel? Do you feel superior or inferior to them?

_____
_____
_____
_____

2. What does another have that you would like to have, or believe you must have, in order be happy? (This could mean another's spouse, house, appearance, abilities, knowledge, power, etc.)

_____
_____
_____
_____

3. What do you believe about yourself which makes you want to have what another has, or be like another? What will happen if that does not happen?

_____
_____
_____
_____

4. Do you feel you are a person of worth, at least on an equal plane as others? If so, what are your best qualities that make you equal to others?

_____
_____
_____
_____

Phase 4 Not Satisfied:

Unfortunately, most of the comparing does not usually make you happy. The reason behind this is found in this statement: Even if you become exactly like the person who is the target of your comparisons you still are not that person. At most, you are a close copy of that person. In a pattern of envy, being a close copy of some outside person can cause a great deal of dissatisfaction in the long run. Since you have no idea of your personal identity, you live with this copy of someone else's identity. This may leave you empty inside and looking for your real identity that was abandoned in search of some outside identity.

1. Do you believe life is not giving you exactly what you need to grow and be happy?

_____
_____
_____
_____

2. How often do you feel as though nothing is horribly wrong, but nothing is right either? If often, please describe how you cope with your feelings of dissatisfaction.

_____
_____
_____
_____

3. Do you usually feel secure in the relationships that you maintain in your life? How dependent are you on other people for your own happiness?

_____
_____
_____
_____

4. Have you lost any relationship in your life because of your behavior? If so, what was the behavior that bothered your partner the most?

_____
_____
_____
_____

Phase 5 Buried Anger:

A pattern of envy can be filled with buried anger because even if you wanted to be someone else, deep down inside you know you are not. You may find yourself empty and angry about giving up on yourself. Some drug addicts are like this. They may have started drugs because they thought it would make them cool. Now addicted and with the identity of a drug addict, they may be filled with buried anger for those who are not addicted. The buried anger is based on never quite finding yourself and not being comfortable in your own skin.

1.Have you in the past or recently made nasty comments about or did something negative towards someone who had something or some quality you wished to have?

_____
_____
_____

2. When you see other people's qualities and achievements what negative thoughts come into your mind?

_____
_____
_____
_____

3. Do you think that success is overrated and that sometimes you get satisfaction from putting people down? If so, write an example when you felt that way and what people you let know?

_____
_____
_____
_____

4. Is there anything you would like to communicate with others concerning what you are feeling? If so, what would you like to communicate?

_____
_____
_____
_____

Phase 6 Self Torture:

Instead, a person in an envy pattern may be tortured trying to achieve something that is unachievable. For example, someone with anorexia nervosa is tortured by never being thin enough. No matter what the weight, it is never thin enough. In many ways, these people will never be satisfied with a belief based on some outside image of being thin. Instead they will torture themselves to continue to lose weight. Self-torture only draws you further away from finding your own identity. You may not believe that your personal identity is important until terrible things happen to you and you are left with only yourself. Not knowing yourself at that moment can be devastating.

1. Do you sometimes feel that the society and the culture around you have built much higher standards than you can achieve?

_____
_____
_____
_____

2. Do you sometimes feel the need to escape from your current life?

_____
_____
_____
_____

3. Do you often feel afraid that people will outdo you?

_____
_____
_____
_____

4. When do you feel negatively about others and which beliefs do you need to change to live a better life?

_____
_____
_____
_____

Exercises and Activities to Promote Healthy Emotional Responses

Overcoming envy is like changing any emotional reaction or behavior. It begins with awareness. Awareness allows you to see that the projected stories in your mind are not true.

1. List the cost and benefits of your behaviors:

Cost:

_____
_____

Benefits:

_____
_____

2. Understanding Your Self-esteem: Your self-esteem reflects how you see yourself and value your different qualities. Each of us has positive and negative qualities, but people with low self-esteem tend to focus on the negative ones rather than the positive ones.

Write your positive character traits:

_____
_____
_____

Write your negative character traits:

_____
_____
_____

3. Change Faulty Assumptions in Your Relationship: A relationship may become difficult if you have faulty assumptions about your partner. For example, faulty assumptions are sometimes based on "undivided attention" or "higher expectation." Write a few faulty assumptions and realistic assumptions.

Faulty Assumption: _____
More Realistic Assumption: _____

Faulty Assumption: _____
More Realistic Assumption: _____

Faulty Assumption: _____
More Realistic Assumption: _____

4. Daily Gratitude: To shift your perspective outward and broaden your view, create a gratitude journal. Take time at the end of each day to write down three things you are grateful for, no matter how insignificant they may seem. It could be a smile from a stranger, a call from a friend, a morning walk, finding a new recipe, a compliment at work-- whatever brightened your day. Write a few things, people and qualities you are grateful for in your life:

_____
_____
_____
_____

5.Imagine your best possible self: This exercise can encourage optimism and positive thinking. Write down a few thoughts below:

_____
_____
_____
_____

6. See How Others Value You: Make a list of people who love and value you and find out how they view you as a person. For example, your mother, father, siblings, friends, mentor and teachers, etc.

_____
_____
_____
_____

7. What does this poem mean to you? It could mean nothing, or it may be a place to start (Express yourself verbally or artistically; write a poem, draw a picture, write a song. Sometimes artistic expression reveals information from our unconscious that has not risen to a conscious level.) Talk about this artistic expression with someone who cares about you.

Envy
The mirror tells my friends
"I am not good enough!"
I live in a mirror of not good enough.
Distracting me from myself, reflecting
the minds of others.

The mirror narrates my life.
I hide from its reflections
while it tells a story of someone else.
I call it, "The Cancer of the Looking Glass"
As I search for the magic cure within myself

The world is a looking glass
"Please leave me alone!"
Somewhere outside the mirror
lies a frightened me
waiting to be discovered

Possibilities in Therapy

Here are some of the suggestions from counselors, psychologists and psychiatrists that over the years have given input into this emotional map.

Phase 1 Outside Pressure:

A therapist may use Narrative Therapy to understand the outside pressures that are causing you to feel this way. Behavioral Therapy may be used to make changes. Structural Family Therapy would be helpful to understand dysfunctional interpersonal rules.

Phase 2 Identity Crisis:

A therapist may use Existential Therapy and ask you to discuss your beliefs that are forming your identity and work on the clarification of your values. Cognitive Behavioral Therapy may be used to make positive changes in your behavior.

Phase 3 Compare:

The loss of locus of control may be responsible for this negative emotion. Person-Centered Therapy may be helpful for your therapist to understand why it is important for you to constantly compare yourself to others. Behavioral Therapy and Solution Based Brief Therapy may be use by your therapist to help you with learning positive behavior and finding a solution to an existing problem.

Phase 4 Not Satisfied:

Your therapist may use Existential Therapy and discuss your beliefs and point out what beliefs are behind your dissatisfaction. Cognitive Therapy may be used to treat negative thoughts.

Phase 5 Buried Anger:

Person Centered therapy is helpful for establishing a strong therapeutic alliance. After forming a positive therapeutic relationship with your therapist, you may feel comfortable to discuss the feelings of resentment and anger and would learn the reasons behind not expressing your negative thoughts and feelings. Experiential System Therapy may also be used to treat buried anger. Rational Emotive Therapy is helpful for resolving emotional and behavioral problems and disturbances. By using Gestalt Therapy, the therapist may ask you to role play and express your negative thoughts and emotions.

Phase 6 Self Torture:

Existential Therapy and Direct Decision Therapy may be useful to treat your self-torture and denial because these therapies are based on a philosophic foundation that is not just a means of therapy but also a philosophy of life. Narrative Therapy may be used to explore your beliefs behind torturing yourself. In some cases, sensitivity training may also be used to make you aware of your own faulty thought patterns. The therapist may also discuss your nutritional and medical history.

An Emotional Algorithm for Envy

Here is an emotional algorithm for envy. Again, an emotional algorithm is a procedure or formula for solving a possible problem, based on conducting a sequence of specified actions. This is a starting point in helping you regulate your emotions. Talk about this algorithm with someone who cares about you.

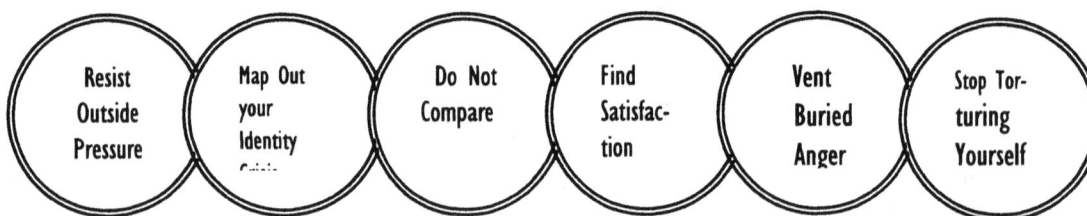

Resist Outside Pressure → Map Out your Identity Crisis → Do Not Compare → Find Satisfaction → Vent Buried Anger → Stop Torturing Yourself

Figure 6.2

Reader's Personalized Emotional Map for Envy

Now it is your turn to give direction to regulating your emotions.

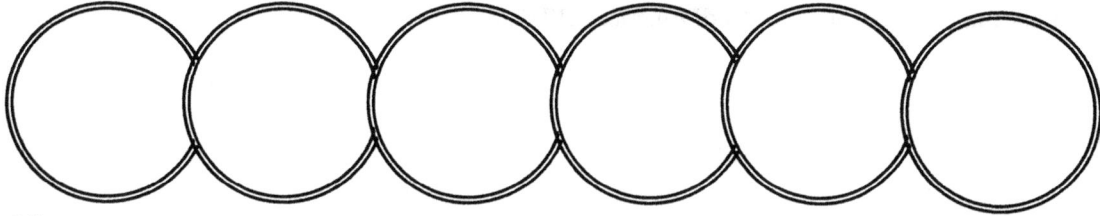

Figure 6.3

Reader's Personalized Action Plan for Emotionally Regulating Envy

-
-
-
-
-
-

Notes

1. Also in Ladd, P.D (2009), *Emotional addictions: A reference book for addictions and mental health counselors.* Lanham, MD: University Press of America. 217–238.

Chapter 7: Guilt

Introduction to Guilt

Guilt is an emotion that dates back to when people started judging each other. In other words, guilt has been around for a long time. Some people might say that guilt is not an emotion but a judgment. That may be true for the person doing the judging, but for the judged, it is sometimes filled with regret, blame and shame. Take for example the alcoholic parent who hardly ever gives his or her children a compliment. Picture a young student coming home with a report card of all A's and one B. For many of us, we would see that as an excellent job, but for the alcoholic parent it may be an opportunity to say, "It is not good enough." The alcoholic parent feels he or she will lose control if praise is given. By saying "It is not good enough." the student may feel guilty for not meeting the expectations of someone who needs control over life circumstances.

Also, sometimes we confuse guilt with sadness. Sadness is an emotion that expresses how we feel, usually when we are experiencing loss. During the process of grieving sadness helps us emotionally move on from our grief. With loss, sadness is an appropriate response. On the other hand, many of us confuse sadness with guilt. Guilt puts a negative judgment on our sadness, again causing us the potential for regret, blame and shame.

One other reason to understand the workings of guilt lies in its power to control people. Take for example the alcoholic father where the children never could do enough to receive praise. By guilt "tripping" the children, he can more easily control them. They may be constantly working for his acceptance. Think about the number of times you have experienced guilt as a way for others to control you.[1]

In this chapter, the stages of guilt will be mapped out so a clearer understanding can be made of this powerful emotion. At times, all of us feel we have done something wrong, especially if we have high-standards for living a structured life, where breaking the rules have their consequences. Understand where guilt fits into your life. Is it an emotion that holds you back from succeeding in your goals, or does some guilt help you stay on track for what you are trying to accomplish?

Emotional Pattern for Guilt

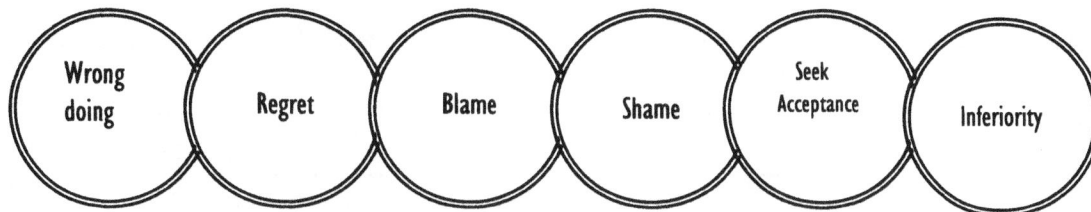

Figure 7.1

Phase 1 Wrong Doing:

Sometimes you can find yourself feeling that something is wrong even though it may be difficult to isolate why you feel this way. For example, this can happen in a school classroom where the teacher makes everyone feel guilty. As soon as the teacher walks in the door, students may feel guilt from the judgmental stare of the teacher. A pattern of guilt can be very subtle in this case. Other times, you just feel that something is wrong but you cannot pinpoint its source. You anticipate how others make you feel guilty or you have certain situations in your life where you make yourself guilty. A common example is sexual abuse as a child even though it was not the child's fault.

1. Think about what makes you feel that you have done something wrong? Give three examples, and try to identify the feelings you have/had when you have/had negative thoughts of self-doubt and wrong doing.

_____
_____
_____
_____

2. How often do you feel that you have done something wrong, even though you know you haven't? If often, please describe how you cope with this feeling.

_____
_____
_____
_____

3. What are the events, situations, or thoughts that trigger some level of self-doubt?

_____
_____
_____
_____

4. Are there people in your life who are responsible for triggering self-doubt in you? If so, please describe who they are and how they make you feel this way.

_____
_____
_____
_____

Phase 2 Regret:

In a pattern of guilt, the more aware you are of doing something wrong the more clearly you regret your actions. If you do something wrong and then specifically know what it was that you did wrong, then you can change those regrettable behaviors into something positive. All of us eventually do things wrong according to someone's point of view. If you change these regrets into something positive then regret can be a positive learning experience. That is how people make amends or at least stop doing things wrong. Unfortunately, in a pattern of guilt, you may regret something yet may not get specific enough to change the wrong doing.

1. Looking back at your life so far, are you happy with how it turned out or do you have any regrets? If you have regrets what are they? Consider writing down at least three regrets you have in your life.

_____
_____
_____
_____

2. Do you dwell on these regrets? Is there anything you could have done to change the outcome? If so, please describe what you would have done differently.

_____
_____
_____
_____

3. How have those regrets impacted your present life?

_____
_____
_____

4. Do you think you can change your regrets into something positive?

_____
_____
_____
_____

Phase 3 Blame:

If you are in a pattern of guilt and have not resolved your regrets, you may start blaming yourself and to make matters worse, you may get help from others who also want to blame you. Now you are not having regrets about something you did but you are blaming yourself for what you *do* wrong. Remember, this is a crucial shift in your thinking. When you were regretting, it was something you *did* that was wrong. Now it is *what you do* that is wrong. We all have done things wrong but that does not mean we are bad people. When you blame yourself, you say, "I am a bad person."

1. Do you have a powerful inner critic who finds fault with nearly everything you do? If so, please write down a few self-blaming statements you repeat in your mind.

_____
_____
_____
_____

2. Do you always blame yourself if something goes wrong in a relationship? If so, please give an example.

_____
_____
_____
_____

3. Do you believe you make it difficult for people in your life to love you?

_____
_____
_____
_____

4. Do you believe you were a disappointment to your parents, children, partner, or to your whole family?

_____
_____
_____
_____

Phase 4 Shame:

Here is how in a pattern of guilt, people go from thinking they do bad-things to becoming bad people, at least in their own minds. If you have done what you consider a bad-thing it does not make you a bad person. If you blame yourself for being a bad person then soon you may feel ashamed. Shame is what you feel when you judge yourself as a bad person. Feeling shame can have a lasting effect on your identity. In a pattern of guilt, you begin to identify yourself with something wrong or bad and feel ashamed. In some respects, you condemn yourself or you let others condemn you. Either way, you dramatically change the way you are going to look at yourself. Anytime, you feel ashamed it may add to a negative view of yourself.

1. Do you consider yourself a good person who does the right thing? If yes, why? If no, why not?

_____
_____
_____
_____

2. Are you a perfectionist? If so, how do you feel when you don't achieve perfection in anything you do?

_____
_____
_____
_____

3. What makes you feel ashamed? Give some examples, and try to identify the feeling you have when you have shame.

_____
_____
_____
_____

4. Do you ever feel ashamed when you are not supposed to?

_____
_____
_____
_____

Phase 5 Seek Acceptance:

Feeling ashamed makes you an easy mark for those who want to hurt you. But instead of defending yourself you may seek acceptance from the people who initially put you down. You may find yourself constantly seeking acceptance to balance out your shame. Unfortunately, some people will take advantage of your need for acceptance and blame you for more wrong doing. This is how, for example, young children take physical abuse from a battering parent yet they still seek the parent's acceptance. Even though the parent controls these children through guilt tripping, these children will still seek the parent's acceptance.

1. What negative messages did your parents or other adults in your life give to you when you were growing up?

_____
_____
_____
_____

2. Do you believe the only way someone can like you is if you do what they want? If so, please elaborate.

_____
_____
_____
_____

3. How do other people use "guilt trips" to manipulate you?

_____
_____
_____

4. Is there anything that you are having trouble forgiving yourself for?

_____
_____
_____
_____

Phase 6 Inferiority:

If anyone wonders why some people feel inferior to others, then the pattern of guilt is a good example. If you believe you deserve to be ashamed and you seek acceptance from those who make you feel ashamed, then how can you possibly feel good about yourself under those conditions? Of course, the pattern of guilt is not finished. Now that you feel inferior, you can go back to Phase 1 and feel more wrong and regret. In many ways, a pattern of guilt can create a rut that is hard to overcome. Between regret, blame, and shame you are slowly losing your self-esteem; between a need for acceptance and feeling inferior you are losing your self-confidence.

1. What are the traits you most dislike in yourself?

_____
_____
_____
_____

2. Do you try to hide your flaws or distract people from them without success?

_____
_____
_____
_____

3. Do you often apologize for things that are not your fault?

_____
_____
_____
_____

4. Have you ever noticed that sometimes people take advantage of you or abuse you? If yes, please write the following: When was the last time you noticed that happening? How does that make you feel?

_____
_____
_____
_____

Exercises and Activities to Promote Healthy Emotional Responses

Excessive guilt is one of the biggest destroyers of self-esteem, individuality, creativity and personal development. The past cannot be changed, no matter how you feel about it. Excessive guilt will neither alter the past nor make you a better person.

1. List the cost and benefits of your behaviors:

Cost:

_____
_____

Benefits:

_____
_____

2. Recognize your negative self-talk: What we say or think about ourselves has a real impact. Often, outside factors are blamed, but it's really our interpretation of the situation that has caused our reaction. Write a few negative self-talks or maintain a similar journal to record your negative self-talk.

Situation_____
Resulting Self-talk_____
Resulting feeling/emotions_____
Rational rsponse_____

3. List your character traits:

Positive character traits: Negative character traits:

_____   _____
_____   _____
_____   _____
_____   _____

4. Change your perception about you: Distinguish between how you think about an experience and the facts surrounding the experience.

a) Reflect on five predominant symptoms that negatively affect you. For example, self-blaming; "I am so stupid."

_____

_____

b) Identify a recent event that you feel was caused by the symptom e.g., "I didn't do well in my recent exam."

_____

_____

c) Identify the factual event. For example: "I missed several classes."

_____

_____

5. Consider the positive messages you wish you heard as a child?

_____

_____

_____

_____

6. Accept your mistakes and move on: Give one example.

Your mistake: _____

_____

What did you learn from your mistake: _____

_____

7. What does this poem mean to you? It could mean nothing, or it may be a place to start (Express yourself verbally or artistically; write a poem, draw a picture, write a song. Sometimes artistic expression reveals information from our unconscious that has not risen to a conscious level.) Talk about this artistic expression with someone who cares about you.

Guilt

I feel guilt and all its pain.
Am I worthless, to the point of shame?
Is there forgiveness for the cage you've built?
Can life understand my depth of guilt?
And, is guilt a mark of shame
or imperfection, by any name?
I'm not perfect and neither are you.
So, stop judging what I do
Shame keeps lurking in your mind
Caught in a cage for the emotionally blind
Blind to imperfection, blind to identification
Blind to reconciliation, blind to appreciation
Open your eyes to my unfinished life.
Open your eyes to freedom and forgiveness

Possibilities in Therapy

Here are some of the suggestions from counselors, psychologists and psychiatrists that over the years have given input into this emotional map.

Phase 1 Wrong Doing:

Cognitive Therapy may help you to discuss the thoughts behind subtle acceptance of feeling associated with wrong doing. Your therapist may use Choice Therapy to make you understand that the source of much personal unhappiness is failing or failed relationships with people important to you. Assertive Training is effective to help you to stand up for yourself and to empower you, in more contemporary terms.

Phase 2 Regret:

Cognitive Behavioral Therapy may be used to help you to reflect what thoughts are causing regretful behavior. Rational Emotive Therapy would be helpful in resolving emotional and behavioral problems and disturbances.

Phase 3 Blame:

A therapist may explore what beliefs are causing compulsive self-blame behavior. Cognitive Behavioral Therapy may develop critical thinking and make you understand your irrational self-blame behavior. Your therapist may use Solution Focused Therapy to observe and explore your behavior and thought patterns.

Phase 4 Shame:

A therapist may explore your social situation which is causing shame. Your therapist may use Psychoanalysis to explore your social inferiority and why it is acceptable for you to live with the feeling of shame. Existential therapy and Direct Decision Therapy may be helpful to understand your philosophy of life and find ways to change your negative mindset.

Phase 5 Acceptance:

A therapist may explore your thinking which may make you constantly seek acceptance. Family Therapy may be helpful if you deal with attention vs. care issues. Cognitive Behavioral Therapy would be helpful to change your negative thought patterns.

Phase 6 Acceptance:

Your therapist may discuss and explore your beliefs behind your feelings of inferiority and how that affects an addictive cycle of guilt. Assertiveness training may be helpful to treat your inferiority. Existential Therapy would help to clarify your values and beliefs.

An Emotional Algorithm for Guilt

Here is an emotional algorithm for guilt. Again, an emotional algorithm is a procedure or formula for solving a possible problem, based on conducting a sequence of specified actions. This is a starting point in helping you regulate your emotions. Talk about this algorithm with someone who cares about you.

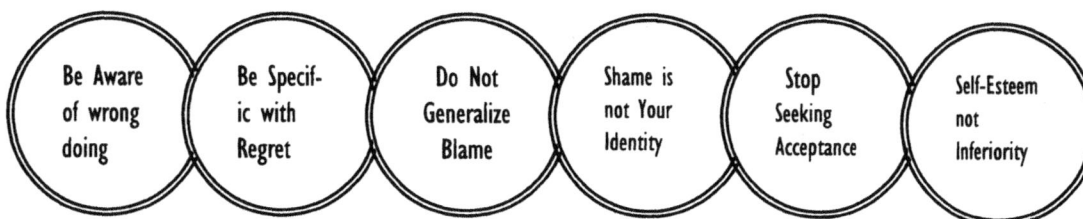

Figure 7.2

Reader's Personalized Emotional Algorithm for Guilt

Now it is your turn to give direction to regulating your emotions

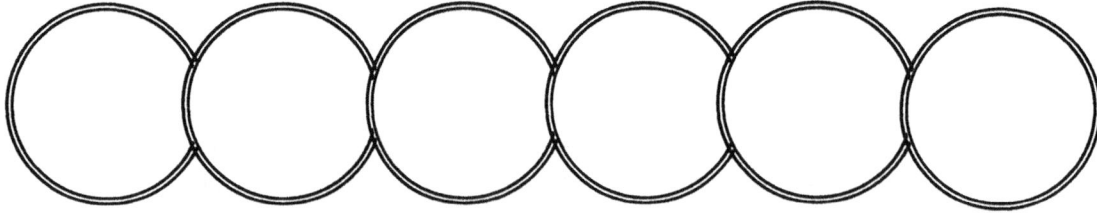

Figure 7.3

Reader's Personalized Action Plan for Emotionally Regulating Guilt

-
-
-
-
-
-

Notes

    1. Information for including others can be found in the following book., Blanchfield, K. E., & Ladd, P. D. (2013*). Leadership, violence and school climate: Case studies in creating non-violent schools.* Lanham, MD: Rowman & Littlefield Education. 215—227.

Chapter 8: Jealousy

Introduction to Jealousy

Jealousy is different than an emotion such as envy, in some subtle ways. Envy is about not having something and envying those who have it, whether it is money, popularity, or looks. On the other hand, jealousy is about having something and fearing that someone else will take it from you. Keeping this in mind, we may experience mild cases of jealousy in our lives when life makes a change and what we thought was securely our own is threatened by another. The typical example is the boyfriend or girlfriend where either is threatened by an outsider who is attracted to one of them.

Yet, the fear of losing a partner is just one possibility when experiencing jealousy. Take for example, professional jealousy where you feel secure at your job until a newcomer threatens to do a better job, or a child who feels jealousy when a new baby is born into the family. These examples start with a certain type of fear that leads to the emotion of jealousy. In many ways, it is the fear of losing something that makes us consider going through a jealous experience.

It is hard to say whether jealousy is inherent in our lives. Some professionals believe it is a part of our biology (Robbie-Gillet, Howard and McCarthy 2012). Others believe it is a learned behavior, (Lewis 2016) where we are taught to be protective of our possessions. In either case, words like "protecting one's turf, or "possessive love" seem a part of our vocabulary. In this chapter, you have a chance to discover whether there are moments where a fear of losing something is important in your life. Or, whether that fear is ongoing— bringing up the potential for protecting your possessions at all costs, to the point of using force. In some respects, a pattern of jealousy is like playing poker. If you fear losing something, you may continue to "up the ante" until what is yours is protected. In this manner, jealousy can get out of hand.

Emotional Pattern of Jealousy

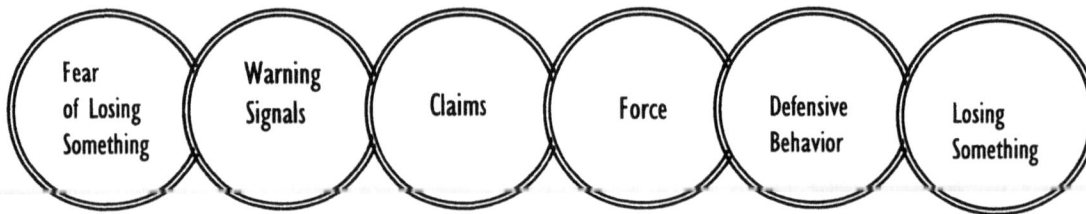

Figure 8.1

Phase 1 Fear of Losing Something:

A pattern of jealousy is based on a fear of losing something. There are numerous things one may be afraid of losing. For example, a fear of losing face, a fear of losing control or power, a fear of losing another person and the list goes on. Some people are more territorial than others and when someone steps into their territory they become afraid that something will be lost. Jealousy works from the belief that certain things are mine such as a significant other, or a specific job. On occasions, our culture subtly says these people or things are a part of what we protect so, for example, if someone comes up to your girlfriend or boyfriend and tries to flirt with them, you may experience a certain fear of losing something.

1. Please write down the things you are afraid of losing. It could be an ability, a trait, a quality, a relationship, a cultural aspect, a possession or anything else you value the most.

_____
_____
_____
_____

2. What will happen if you lose your "valuable possessions"?

_____
_____
_____
_____

3. Do you sometimes feel you are losing control over your "valuable possessions"? If so, how do you feel at that moment?

_____
_____
_____
_____

4. What do you do to protect your "valuable possessions"?

_____
_____
_____
_____

Phase 2 Warning signals:

Usually, you do not initially make a big deal about this type of fear. You may send out warning signals to the person threatening you and subtly warn the person to get out of your turf. If the person realizes that he or she is stepping in what you consider your territory and that person backs off, at that point the jealous pattern ends. In our relationships, workplace settings, classrooms and other social areas, you may demonstrate a whole series of warning signals that can be used to help protect your turf and calm your fears. Some people experiencing a pattern of jealousy can control the behavior of many different people by sending out warning signals when these people step over the line.

1. What are your warning signals when you are jealous?

_____
_____
_____
_____

2. Do you feel that people must follow your wishes most of the time? If so, how do you feel when they do not?

_____
_____
_____
_____

3. What is your concept of personal boundaries? Do you think you respect other peoples' personal boundaries?

_____
_____
_____
_____

4. Think about how you stop people when you think they are threatening your territory, possessions, quality traits, cultural aspects or relationships?

_____
_____
_____
_____

Phase 3 Claims:

A pattern of jealousy can escalate to more serious behavior. Sometimes a jealous person who has made numerous warning signals may escalate his or her behavior by making a claim. A jealous claim takes many forms but basically it goes beyond just warning signals and is a direct claim that the person or thing belongs to you. For example, if someone at work starts to do a part of your job, you might tell that person that it is my work, not yours. Usually, this is the first sign that a person is jealous when they put in a jealous claim. At this point, people usually know a claim is being made. You are claiming your territory, possession or person.

1. Do you devote a lot of attention and energy to keeping your personal environment organized according to your own preference? If so, what happens when someone disrupts it?

_____
_____
_____
_____

2. Do you give people a lot of directives, unsolicited advice, suggestions, and "constructive criticism?"

_____
_____
_____
_____

3. Do you have lots of personal rules, routines, rituals, and ceremonies?

_____
_____
_____
_____

4. Do you dislike accepting help from people at work or elsewhere, or allowing them to do things for you? If so, how do you feel when people help you out with work and responsibilities assigned to you?

_____
_____
_____
_____

Phase 4 Force:

If the warning signal does not work and the claim does not work, then you may use force to get back what you believe is your possession. One example of using force in jealousy is in child abuse or some forms of battering. Jealous people feel justified in using force because they are fighting for their possessions. Someone who hits one of their lover's children might say, "Well I warned him." Jealous people usually may not feel they are doing anything wrong when they use force, because their belief is that they are protecting what they own.

1. Do you believe that people in your house should follow your rules? If so, how do you make them do that?

_____
_____
_____
_____

2. Is the easiest emotion for you to show anger or irritability when you are afraid of losing one of your "possessions"? If so, how do you express your anger and irritability?

_____
_____
_____
_____

3. Do you have a logical explanation for the way you act, even if others cannot always accept it? If so, write down an example when you thought you were right in acting the way you did but other people involved got upset.

_____
_____
_____
_____

4. Have you ever used physical force, verbal threats of using force, or emotional threats to keep your loved ones from doing something against your wishes?

_____
_____
_____
_____

Phase 5 Defensive Behavior:

Jealous people may defend their actions as justified to protect their possessions. This makes a pattern of jealousy difficult to resolve. If you used force and later said you knew that it was wrong, then the ability to stop using force would be easier to change in your behavior. However, in a pattern of jealousy, you may feel justified in using force and sometimes you may get help from the person you are possessing. For example, if you ask some battered women why they let a boyfriend beat them up when they go into a jealous rage, that girlfriend might just say, "My boyfriend's behavior is not jealousy but possessive love." Unfortunately, her analysis of the situation is wrong. She has confused jealousy with love.

1. Do you sometimes find it difficult to convince people who are close to you that you have their best interest in mind, when stopping them from doing something?

_____
_____
_____
_____

2. Have you ever tried to minimize your unacceptable behavior and explained the reason why you treated the other person(s) the way you did or made excuses, rationalizations and blames? If so, write an example.

_____
_____
_____
_____

3. What are the feelings you have or the thoughts that come into your mind when you try to convince other people to believe you?

_____
_____
_____
_____

4. Have you ever shifted responsibility for your actions away from yourself and onto others? A shift that allowed you to justify your actions because the other person(s) supposedly "caused" your "behavior"?

_____
_____
_____
_____

Phase 6 Losing Something:

A jealous rage does not stop you from feeling something is being lost. In a pattern of jealousy, using force and then acting defensively does not diminish your fear of losing something. Using claims, force and defensive behavior seems to make you more afraid of losing something and not lessen your fear. The pattern of jealousy starts with a fear of losing something that eventually may end in losing something. If you have a fear of losing something, it may be better to find ways that do not include using warning signal, claims or force.

1. Have your loved ones or anyone else in your life complained about your insecure behavior? If so, what do they say? Give some examples.

_____
_____
_____
_____

2. Do you feel you are not appreciated by those who care for you? If so, how does that make you feel?

_____
_____
_____
_____

3. Are you over-concerned and worried that people around you would get fed up with your behavior and leave you or keep a distance from you? If so, write some of the thoughts that come to your mind.

_____
_____
_____
_____

4. Is there anything you would like to communicate to others concerning what you are feeling? What would you like to communicate?

_____
_____
_____
_____

Exercises and Activities to Promote Healthy Emotional Responses

Overcoming jealousy is like changing any emotional reaction or behavior. It begins with awareness. Awareness allows you to see that the projected stories in your mind are not true.

1. List the cost and benefits of your behaviors:

Cost:

_____
_____
_____

Benefits: _____
_____
_____

2. Understanding Your Self-esteem: Your self-esteem reflects how you see yourself and value your different qualities. Each of us has positive and negative qualities, but people with low self-esteem tend to focus on the negative ones rather than the positive ones.

Write your positive character traits:_____
_____
_____
_____

Write your negative character traits: _____
_____
_____
_____

3. Change Faulty Assumptions in Your Relationships: A relationship may become difficult if you have faulty assumptions about your partner. For example, faulty assumptions are sometimes based on "undivided attention" or "higher expectation." Write a few faulty assumptions and realistic assumptions.

Faulty Assumption: _____
More Realistic Assumption: _____
Faulty Assumption: _____
More Realistic Assumption: _____

4. Keep Track of Your Negative Self Talk:

Negative self-talk adversely affects your feelings and choices and overall way of life more than most people realize. What we say or think to ourselves has a real impact. Often, outside factors are blamed, but it's really our interpretation of the situation that has caused our reaction.

Make the similar columns in your journal and track your negative self-talk.

Situation:
_____
_____

Rational Response:
_____
_____

5. See How Others Value You: Make a list of people who love and value you and find out how they view you as a person. For example, your mother, father, siblings, friends, mentor and teachers, etc.
_____
_____
_____
_____

6. Daily Gratitude: To shift your perspective outward and broaden your view, think about creating a gratitude journal. Take time at the end of each day to write down three things you are grateful for, no matter how insignificant you think they are. It could be a smile from a stranger, a call from a friend, a morning walk, finding a new recipe, a compliment at work— whatever brightened your day. Write a few things, people and qualities you are grateful for in your life:
_____
_____
_____
_____

7. What does this poem mean to you? It could mean nothing, or it may be a place to start (Express yourself verbally or artistically; write a poem, draw a picture, write a song. Sometimes artistic expression reveals information from our unconscious that has not risen to a conscious level.) Talk about this artistic expression with someone who cares about you.

Jealousy

I am confused
Does he love me?
Why am I so lonely?
Is jealousy a part of love?
These are the questions that
haunt me with each smothering embrace.
They feel like chains that wrap around my life
It must be love. It must be love. I'll make it love.

Possibilities in Therapy

Here are some of the suggestions from counsellors, psychologists and psychiatrists that over the years have given input into this emotional map.

Phase 1 Fear of losing something:

The therapist may ask you to describe your social world and environment and what would make you afraid of losing something. The therapist may use Structural System Therapy (Social system and boundaries) as well as Cognitive Behavioral Therapy; such as mediation.

Phase 2 Warning signals:

The therapist may ask you to describe some of the triggers of warning signals. Behavioral therapy like relaxation techniques and meditation may help when you feel threatened.

Phase 3 Claims:

The therapist may ask you to discuss in depth your social life and environment that is causing you to claim; power turf etc. Mediation, like finding common ground may be used to ease up the tension. Solution Focused Therapy and Structural System Therapy are effective to understand and build boundaries.

Phase 4 Force:

You may have to discuss what behavior or feelings are leading you to use force. Behavioral Therapy for Anger Management is effective if there are abuse issues. Venting is therapeutic therefore Gestalt Therapy and Person-Centered Therapy would be helpful.

Phase 5 Defensive Behavior:

Thoughts that are leading to defensive behavior and addictive thinking may be discussed. Conciliation skills and reframing may also be used by your therapist. Cognitive Behavioral Therapy and Choice Therapy are effective for defensive behavior and addictive thinking.

Phase 6 Losing Something:

The therapist may discuss the sense of loss you feel while practicing this emotional pattern. Grief counseling is effective if you have experienced loss. Person Centered Therapy and Assertiveness Training may help to have a fresh start.

An Emotional Algorithm for Jealousy

Here is an algorithm for Jealousy. Again, an algorithm is a procedure or formula for solving a possible problem, based on conducting a sequence of specified actions. This is a starting point in helping you regulate your emotions. Talk about this algorithm with someone who cares about you.

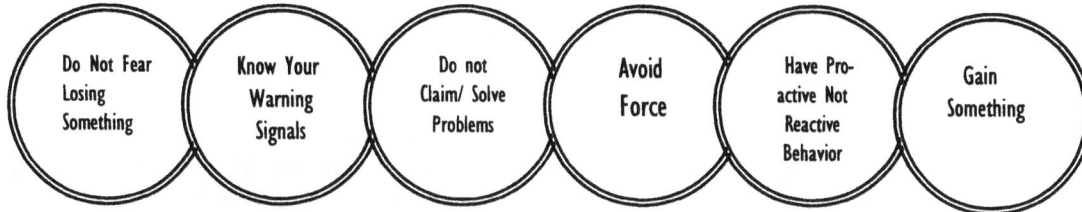

Do Not Fear Losing Something — Know Your Warning Signals — Do not Claim/ Solve Problems — Avoid Force — Have Pro-active Not Reactive Behavior — Gain Something

Figure 8.2

Reader's Personalized Emotional Algorithm for Jealousy

Now it is your turn to give direction to regulating your emotions

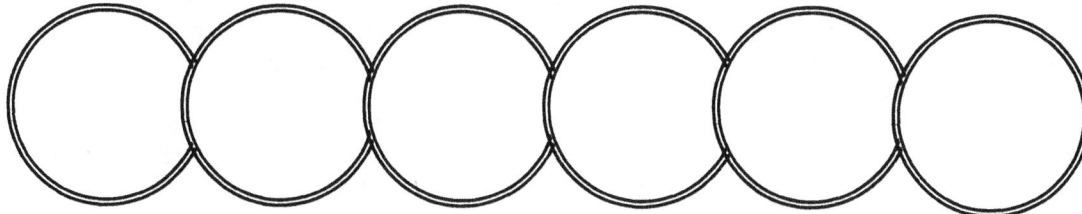

Figure 8.3

Reader's Personalized Action Plan for Emotionally Regulating Jealousy.

-
-
-
-
-
-

Chapter 9: Loneliness

Introduction

The idea of not experiencing loneliness at some point in one's life seems a bit remarkable. There are too many variables where being lonely becomes an appropriate response to a given situation. For example, it may be that loneliness is a necessary part of being in love (Moustakas 1994). When you are with someone you love, the chances of being lonely greatly diminish. However, when in love and not with that person the chances of loneliness greatly increase. This also applies to yourself. If you are not in touch with yourself, it may be difficult to be alone. You may need someone to take away the loneliness. The idea of being alone when you are comfortable with yourself can become a real possibility, even an event you look forward to having. That does not mean that people who are alone are comfortable with it. Some people are alone because life has found a way of isolating them from others.

Another point to consider is that loneliness may eventually cause depression but it is not in itself depression. Loneliness is more connected to feeling isolated from others rather than based on a lack of pleasure. Unfortunately, there are mental health professionals who treat them the same, even though they are not the same. Loneliness is much more connected to relationships with others in the social world where as depression has more biological connections than does loneliness. Yet, both seem to isolate the person from others and that may be the connection that makes them appear the same.

In this chapter, you will find that loneliness is not necessarily bad. If handled correctly, loneliness can be used to clarify what you want out of life. It is the ability to be with others or not be with them, that the experience of loneliness can help clarify. It is when you are lonely and it becomes difficult to connect with the social world then loneliness can be painful. You see this in addiction. Some people deal with their loneliness and the pain that comes with it by taking pain relievers. How many drug addicted people started out taking drugs based on the pain that comes with loneliness? A more important question may be, how do you deal with loneliness? Is it a painful curse that isolates you from others, or is loneliness the great clarifier of what you find meaningful in life? Do you have a need to be constantly with others to avoid loneliness? These are questions that hopefully can be answered in this chapter.

Emotional Pattern of Loneliness

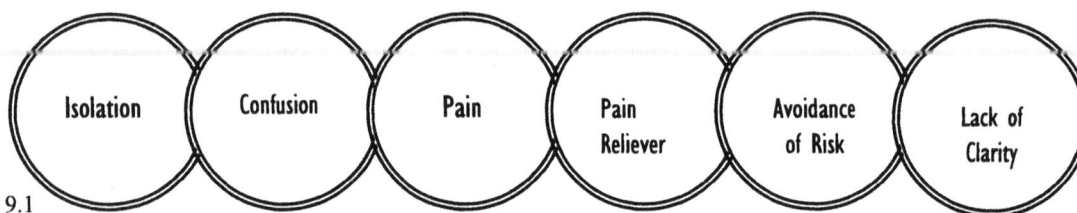

Figure 9.1

Phase 1 Isolation:

Unless you are lucky, there seems to be little chance that you can avoid loneliness through an entire lifetime. There is a difference between loneliness and wanting to be alone. When you want to be alone, it may be for peace and quiet or it may be to gather your thoughts and have some time off from a busy everyday life. Loneliness is different than wanting to be alone. It is not something you seek out for peace or quiet. Loneliness begins with feeling isolated from others. You feel disconnected. Even if you are with people you may feel isolated from them. This isolation can happen for different reasons. You may have loved someone and now that person is gone or you may have been unable to find a lover in the first place. Though loneliness and love seem to have connections, you also can feel isolated for other reasons such as; becoming ill, unresolved conflict, unresolved dreams, difficulty in socializing and so forth.

1. Do you sometimes feel that no one knows you well? If so, describe your impression on people around you.

_____
_____
_____
_____

2. How do you feel when you are alone? For example, do you feel at peace or do you feel unhappy being alone? Please describe in a few sentences.

_____
_____
_____
_____

3. Do you feel you are in tune with people around you or you feel left out? Please describe your feelings?

_____
_____
_____
_____

4. Do you often have this feeling that your social relationships are superficial? If so, how does that make you feel?

_____
_____
_____
_____

Phase 2 Confusion:

Being isolated from others can be very confusing. Since you are not connected to them, in some respects you have to guess as to what is needed in order to get connected to them. Feeling isolated usually does not make your guesses easy. It may cause you confusion as to how you should fit into your life or how you should fit into the lives of others around you. Unfortunately, your confusion may not at first help you feel any less isolated. Trying to fit in, may do the opposite. It may make you feel more isolated and confused. The confusion of feeling isolated may not improve your confidence nor may it help in making you feel connected. It is a stage in loneliness where a lot of "soul searching" can go on. For example, "Who am I?" or "What am I doing here?" These are the types of questions that seem to come up when you are isolated and confused.

1. Do you sometimes feel confused about your own identity and your goals in life? If so, explain some of the thoughts that come to your mind when you are at that state of mind.

_____
_____
_____
_____

2. Do you sometimes feel that people are around you but not with you? If so, what do you do to get accepted and get connected with people?

_____
_____
_____
_____

3. Do you feel comfortable being yourself around others? If you don't, please explain what would happen if others saw the real you?

_____
_____
_____
_____

4. Do you often find it difficult to make friends? If so, explain your thoughts and feeling when you feel disappointment in your ability to make friends.

_____
_____
_____
_____

Phase 3 Pain:

It is the inability to find meaning in life that eventually causes you pain. Pain and loneliness seem to be closely connected. Some people describe this pain as feeling meaningless inside and aching from a sense of emptiness. Your isolation and confusion does not seem to help with this type of pain. It may make it more intense when you admit that you are isolated from yourself or others and you are confused about how to connect with yourself and others. Some people describe this pain as an intense feeling that affects everything they do. It is the pain that distracts them from personal projects and even from trying to connect with others. Loneliness starts out with a feeling of isolation that leads to confusion and eventually to pain.

1. How would you describe your emotional pain of loneliness?

_____
_____
_____
_____

2. Do you often keep to yourself or do you try very hard to connect with people? Please explain.

_____
_____
_____
_____

3. How often do you experience rejection from people? If often, please describe your feelings the last time someone rejected you.

_____
_____
_____
_____

4. Is the emotional pain of loneliness distracting you from some of the important goals and projects in your life? If so, how?

_____
_____
_____
_____

Phase 4 Pain Reliever:

At this stage, you have reached the crossroads as to what you are going to do about your loneliness. You should be aware that there are two paths you can take from this point on. The first is to accept the isolation, confusion, and pain and live with it until the opportunity for not being lonely comes along. In many respects, this is the better of the two options because even though you are suffering, you are alive and trying to figure out what you want. The second option seems more popular but not necessarily more beneficial. In the second option, you look for some form of pain reliever to take away your pain. You know of people who use alcohol or drugs to get rid of their loneliness or others who pick the company of anyone rather than be alone. Unfortunately, this option may take away your pain and possibly your isolation (though, maybe not) but it may help with your confusion over why you were lonely in the first place.

1. Do you think you are using pain relievers in the form of drugs and alcohol, negative habits, or patterns of relationships to avoid your emotional pain? If so, please explain your form of pain reliever.

_____
_____
_____
_____

2. Do you easily commit to a relationship even though you think that particular person is not the right one for you? If so, please explain your thoughts when someone interested in you invites you into his or her life.

_____
_____
_____
_____

3. Do you sometimes feel that even the use of pain relievers is not helping you to take away your loneliness? If so, please describe your thoughts and feelings.

_____
_____
_____
_____

4. Do you think that avoiding and using temporary means to deal with your emotional pain has created more problems in your life? If so, how?

_____
_____
_____
_____

Phase 5 Avoidance of Risk:

At this phase, it depends on what option you have chosen in the first place. If you have chosen to take risks and stay with your pain and not see your pain as bad, slowly you may work through that pain. However, if you see your pain as something to avoid at all costs then you may not risk working through that pain. Instead you may reinforce using whatever pain reliever you choose to relieve the initial pain of loneliness or you may develop other pain relievers to get rid of your pain. In either case, you are learning a pattern of how to avoid your loneliness instead of developing a pattern to work through it.

1. Is it difficult for you to accept that you feel lonely even when you are surrounded by people? If so why?

_____
_____
_____
_____

2. Do you think that you have learned to live with your emotional pain of loneliness? If so, describe your everyday coping skills.

_____
_____
_____
_____

3. Do you think that you have found the best coping skill to deal with your feeling of loneliness? If so, what is it?

_____
_____
_____
_____

4. What would happen if you let go of your "pain relievers"?

_____
_____
_____
_____

Phase 6 Lack of Clarity:

If you have accepted the pain of loneliness and have stayed with it, then eventually surviving being alone can give you clarity to know what is important to you. You may not just pick any available means or "pain relievers" to help you get rid of your loneliness. You can be stronger and clearer as to what you want and what you need and it will reduce the chances of being lonely again. Even if life puts you in a position of being lonely, you may know what to do to survive it. However, if you have gone to the path of pain relief, then getting clarity with your loneliness may be clouded with getting relief from it. That is not to say that you cannot figure out your life by relieving your pain. In means your pain relievers may be making it more difficult to know what you want. They may lead you back to more isolation.

1. Why do you feel a need to seek help at this point in your life to deal with your emotional pain of loneliness?

_____
_____
_____
_____

2. When did you realize that you are trapped in this painful place of loneliness and that no matter what you do you still feel stuck?

_____
_____
_____
_____

3. What are your plans to deal with your emotional pain of loneliness in the future?

_____
_____
_____
_____

4. If you feel clear about your identity then what kind of a person are you and what do you want to be in the future?

_____
_____
_____
_____

Exercises and Activities to Promote Healthy Emotional Response

The more socially and emotionally isolated we become, the more our social skills and relationships tend to decline. It's a fact, like any other skill when unused, our social skills become weaker and our ability to connect and relate can easily get rusty after a period of isolation. Instead of accepting the reality, we blame ourselves when we fail to connect with people around us.

1. Think about your emotional strengths: Many times, we dwell on the problems that we are having and forget about the emotional strengths we already have to overcome these problems. Make a list of your emotional strengths. Examples like, "I am able to love other people" or "I am a flexible person."

_____
_____
_____
_____

2. Remember the Following Rules:

1. Take initiative to meet people
2. Give others the benefit of the doubt
3. Approach people with optimism

3. Build a support system and find people with common interest: Being connected to others is an important part of your mental health and happiness. If you are isolated and want to make more social connections, you will usually have more success when you participate in groups of people with common interests.

4. Record your thoughts, feelings, sensation and memories: Keeping track of your thoughts feelings, sensation and memories that cause, emotional pain. Maintain a journal of:

   a) Painful thoughts/Feelings/Sensation/Memories
   b) What did you do in response?
   c) Outcome: Negative or Positive

5. Think about a specific goal you have for yourself: Write down the first few steps you could take in order to achieve that goal.

_____
_____
_____
_____

6. Daily Gratitude: This exercise would help you to turn thoughts outward and feel grateful every day. At the end of each day, write down three things you are grateful for. It could be anything. For example, a smile from a stranger, a call from a friend, a morning walk, finding a new recipe, a compliment at work, whatever brightened your day. Write three things you are grateful for right now:

   1. _____
   2. _____
   3. _____

7. What does this poem mean to you? It could mean nothing, or it may be a place to start (Express yourself verbally or artistically; write a poem, draw a picture, write a song. Sometimes artistic expression reveals information from our unconscious that has not risen to a conscious level.) Talk about this artistic expression with someone who cares about you.

Loneliness

Oh! Boozy Moon
Excuse Yourself From
The Dancing Clouds
Long Enough
To Help Your
Capsized Earthly Companion
Who Lies Half Hidden
In this Last Dark Alley
Of the Universe

Possibilities in Therapy

Here are some of the suggestions from counsellors, psychologists and psychiatrists that over the years have given input into this emotional map.

Phase 1 Isolation:

Your therapist may explore your specific form of loneliness and discuss whether you are depressed or whether the isolation is geared more towards loneliness. Treatment for loneliness may need some clarification from a holistic approach because loneliness can be genetic or a social phenomenon, and feelings of isolation may be based on either of these variables. The therapist may point out to you how loneliness can have an existential understanding where isolation is a theme that can be filled with meaning in your life.

Phase 2 Confusion:

A therapist may point out that confusion and rejection may be from feelings of isolation, and not based on personal identity. At this phase, your confusion about loneliness may start to form catastrophic or over generalized thinking patterns. Some form of Rational Emotive Behavior Therapy and transitional counseling may help to clarify the confusion.

Phase 3 Pain:

Your therapist may look for connections between the pain of loneliness and your isolation, and confusion, rather than with symptoms from other mental disorders. The therapist may also discuss some form of pain management to treat the pain connected to loneliness. Cognitive Behavioral Therapy would help you to adjust your thinking about your pain because managing pain whether physical or psychological, and developing a sense of control over your pain may be more appropriate then eliminating it. Meditation that specifically focuses on the pain connected to loneliness may help.

Phase 4 Pain Reliever:

At this phase, a therapist may discuss how relieving the pain of loneliness may lead to other problems such as co-dependency or addiction and working through the pain associated with loneliness can add a purpose and meaning to your life. Some form of focusing training may help to limit distraction and learn to focus on the meaning behind your pain of loneliness.

Phase 5 Avoidance of Risk:

A therapist may discuss how you may want to avoid the risk involved in working through your pain because we all believe that all pain is bad, no matter what the source is. Facing one's pain can be a highly creative act that can lead to love and understanding.

Phase 6 Lack of Clarity:

A therapist may use Psychoanalytic Therapy and discuss your childhood experience and how your attachments or lack of attachment is responsible for your pattern of loneliness. Some form of Object Relation brief therapy may help you to understand the importance of discovering connections in relationships and when these relationships end, the possible loneliness you experience from their ending. Relationship counseling may also be necessary to clarify what types of connections you desire to have in your relationships.

An Emotional Algorithm for Loneliness

Here is an algorithm for loneliness. Again, an algorithm is a procedure or formula for solving a possible problem, based on conducting a sequence of specified actions. This is a starting point in helping you regulate your emotions. Talk about this algorithm with someone who cares about you.

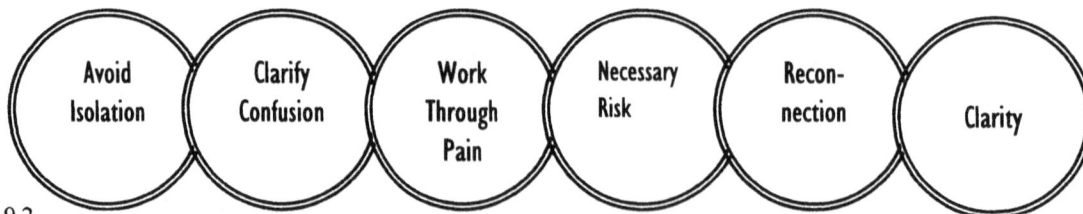

Figure 9.2

Reader's Personalized Emotional Algorithm for Loneliness

Now it is your turn to give direction to regulating your emotions

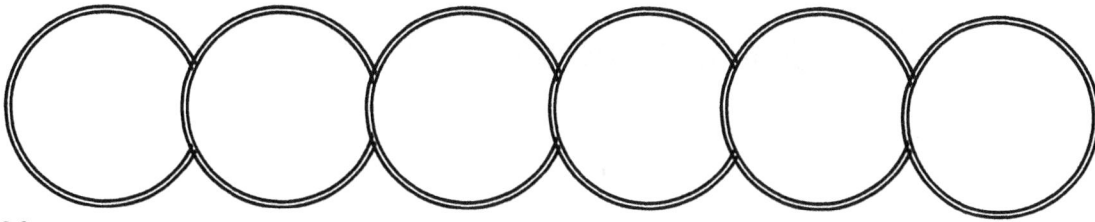

Figure 9.3

Reader's Personalized Action Plan for Emotionally Regulating Loneliness.

-

-

-

-

-

-

Chapter 10: Resentment

Introduction

Some people call resentment civilized anger, where burying it seems more practical than angry explosions dominating our families, workplaces and communities. One of the big differences between anger and resentment is anger being highly visible while resentment is a subtle frustration building over time. It may be this subtle build up that seems to make it more acceptable and civilized. Yet, for those going through the experience of resentment there are some notable side effects. Many resentful people can feel oppressed based on some form of freedom being lost. Take for example, being in a thankless job that you find extremely oppressive, but there are bills to pay and a family to feed. This loss of freedom can cause frustration to slowly build and at some point, you conclude that you are stuck with nowhere to go with your frustration but to bury it.

In some respects, resentment can be more dangerous than anger, especially when that buried frustration rises to the surface. At this point, several things can happen. Built up frustration can turn into a volcano of angry explosions where someone may say, "You need anger management." It may be more accurate to say that anger management techniques are more suitable for resentful people who have finally reached a boiling point. Or, the other pathway for resentment is to turn it into indirect methods of lashing out such as gossip or ambushing others. Again, some may say this is more civilized than open attacks of anger; even though gossip can do as much harm as openly expressing angry outbursts.

In this chapter, you will have the opportunity to separate anger from resentment, along with observing how this pattern slowly can undermine others, where others feel victimized by the experience. You also may find out how popular resentment is as a coping mechanism for one distinct reason, "It works." There is little doubt that when being frustrated over time that talking about others behind their backs takes the edge off one's frustration. Much like an alcoholic takes a drink to take the edge off dealing with problems, so does resentment take the edge off. Unfortunately, like an alcoholic using resentment or taking a drink does not solve your problems. Keeping this in mind, it may be important to spend some time getting to know how resentment works, and see how much it may enter your life. For some, it may come as a surprise how often resentment can be found in everyday living.

Emotional Pattern of Resentment

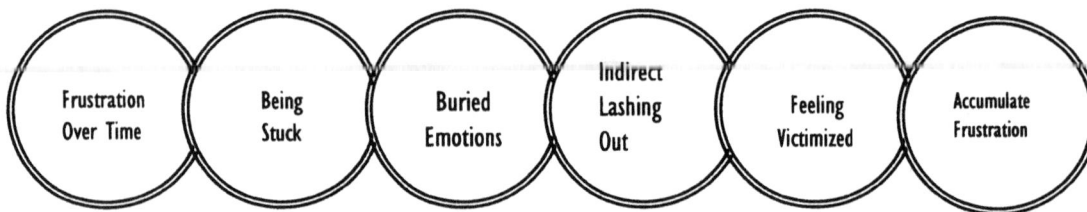

Figure 10.1

Phase 1 Frustration Over Time:

People who develop a pattern of resentment feel frustration over time. This could be frustration over a job, relationship, or any other situation where you feel stuck. What happens is that over time the frustration accumulates and you begin to feel more trapped. Resentment is subtle and it can creep up on you while you remain in a situation that is frustrating. It is the accumulation of frustration that makes you feel oppressed and victimized. For example, some people will live for many years in a relationship that is frustrating, yet they work from the belief that nothing can be done about it. Over time, frustration creates resentment that bogs down many future goals and plans.

1. Do you often feel that life has been unfair to you?

_____
_____
_____
_____

2. Do you think that you have not gotten all the good things that you deserve in life?

_____
_____
_____
_____

3. Do you often feel that there never seems to be enough to go around and you do not seem to get your share?

_____
_____
_____
_____

4. Do you sometimes feel that you never get the advantages that others get?

_____
_____
_____
_____

Phase 2 Being Stuck:

At some point, you could admit to yourself or maybe even to others that certain situations make you feel stuck. Unfortunately, it may be your negative thoughts that force you to feel that way. Ironically, thinking that you are stuck may make you act in ways that keep you stuck. You may not look for ways to un-stick yourself from your frustrating situations. You may accept being stuck and try to make the best of it; even though, deep down inside you are frustrated and possibly angry. You may act as though nothing is wrong while you accumulate more frustration. For example, you may convince yourself that being stuck with an alcoholic partner or a dead-end job is the best you can do for now and maybe for now, you are right.

1. Do you believe that you have had more than your fair share of bad-things coming your way?

_____
_____
_____
_____

2. Do you often think that you never seem to get the breaks or chances that other people do?

_____
_____
_____
_____

3. What is your definition of being "stuck?"

_____
_____
_____

4. Do you believe you are stuck and seriously want to unstick yourself?

_____
_____
_____

Phase 3 Buried Emotions:

So, what are you going to do with all this frustration? Usually in this pattern, you bury it and let it simmer over time. Instead of exploding with anger, you implode with frustration. Sometimes you try to put on a happy face and make the best of it while inside you are feeling frustrated and stuck. For example, many teenagers practice a pattern of resentment when they sit in the classroom, bored with teaching and learning and wishing they could be doing something else. These teenagers may have a great deal of buried frustration that needs to come out. However, if they explode with anger, they may be punished and stay in the classroom even longer. Burying your frustration is a key element in a pattern of resentment.

1. Do you feel controlled by a person, group or organization?

_____
_____
_____
_____

2. Do you dread going into work or the office or anywhere else and deal with controlling people?

_____
_____
_____
_____

3. Do you harbor animosity against someone that you know has wronged you?

_____
_____
_____
_____

4. Is your mind often filled with negative thoughts about breaking out of this dead-end situation?

_____
_____
_____
_____

Phase 4 Indirect Lashing Out:

Eventually, all this frustration does make its way to the surface yet it is usually not in direct forms of anger or aggression. People in a resentful pattern usually lash out indirectly through some form of sarcasm, kidding, gossiping, or just not cooperating with authority. Lashing out indirectly does relieve some of the problem, but it still does not un-stick you from your buried frustration. Many times, it just relieves your frustration on a temporary basis. However, sometimes a resentful pattern will simply cook the frustration and you may erupt like a volcano where everyone is shocked by how angry you have become.

1. Do you often feel suspicious and critical of others who boss you around?

_____
_____
_____
_____

2. Do you feel angry, uneasy, or tense when someone you dislike is mentioned or when you are around that person, and you hide those feelings from that person? Do you indirectly lash out?

_____
_____
_____
_____

3. Do you become easily angered or short-tempered for reasons that make you feel resentful even if you are not consciously aware of the reasons?

_____
_____
_____
_____

4. Do you often engage in harsh conversations about a person, group, or organization and often condemn and criticize that person, group or organization?

_____
_____
_____
_____

Phase 5 Feeling Victimized:

This indirect lashing out, may not solve the frustration problem, so eventually you may feel like a victim of resentment. Unfortunately, feeling like a victim makes you less motivated and less wanting to get involved. Basically, being a victim of resentment means you have lost your freedom and are now stuck without much hope for change. You even may be called lazy or unmotivated. A pattern of resentment may cause you to look lazy or bored when in fact you are stuck. Feeling resentful may cause anger to eventually surface even if you don't normally show your anger. If you explode with anger, it is because it has been accumulating over time and finally it came out.

1. Do you feel that, because of what you've gone through in life, you really feel oppression from the past?

_____
_____
_____
_____

2. When was the last time you felt free to do what you want?

_____
_____
_____
_____

3. Do you often feel the negative effects of bad-things that happened?

_____
_____
_____
_____

4. Does it seem like people have frequently tried to impede your progress?

_____
_____
_____
_____

Phase 6 Accumulating Frustration:

Unfortunately, resentment can accumulate for quite some time without you doing anything about it. Most civilized people would rather deal with resentment than anger. Angry explosions seem to scare people but resentful implosions just seem to hurt the resentful person and possibly cause minor disruption for brief periods of time. From a personal point of view, resentment is probably more dangerous than anger. At least with anger, you know when you are angry. When you are resentful, it is hard to tell whether you are putting on a happy face to cover up your frustration or are you happy? Anger may be a dramatic problem, but resentment can cause hundreds of little problems that eventually may frustrate you.

1. Is your mind often filled with negative thoughts about someone specific or a past event?

_____

_____

_____

_____

2. Do you feel that you were entitled to something that never came your way?

_____

_____

_____

_____

3. Do you feel life has ripped you off? If so. when was the last time you felt this way?

_____

_____

_____

_____

4. If resentful, do you sometimes wonder why you feel so bitter about things?

_____

_____

_____

_____

Exercises and Activities to Promote Healthy Emotional Response

Emotional intelligence begins with learning to recognize your emotions and the effect your emotions have on your behavior, particularly when you are upset.

1. Identify Your Support System: When we are upset it is important to talk to someone. Whether we realize it or not, there are many people in our lives who can give us help and support. Write down names of a few people who would help and support you.

_____

_____

_____

2. Acknowledge and recognize your negative thoughts and feelings: By acknowledging and recognizing your negative thoughts and feelings, you may increase your awareness of the present moment while being non-judgmental, which is important for taking control of your resentful thoughts and feelings. When you take control of your negative thoughts, it will become easier for you to change them.

_____

_____

_____

3. Emotions below the surface: You may have many emotions that you keep below the surface and don't show to others. It would be therapeutic to make a list of your buried emotions and recognize them. Make a list of your buried emotions like sadness, shame, embarrassment, anger etc.

_____

_____

_____

_____

4. Values clarification: Write down the messages you received as a child about your personal values. What are your personal values now?

Messages you received about your personal values: _____

_____

_____

_____

Your personal values: _____

_____

_____

_____

5. Learn to accept reality: Difficulties in your past, present, and future. Your distorted thinking in the past, present, and future.

Reality in the past, present, and future. Take a separate worksheet for each part of your life.

- Past worksheets will help you to accept difficult things from your past.
- Present worksheets will help you to accept difficult things in the present.
- Future worksheets will help you to see ways you can act to help determine your future.

6. Learn self-soothing activities, for example:

    a) Mindfulness meditation
    b) Nature-walk
    c) Calming music
    d) Whatever works best for you

7. What does this poem mean to you? It could mean nothing, or it may be a place to start (Express yourself verbally or artistically; write a poem, draw a picture, write a song. Sometimes artistic expression reveals information from our unconscious that has not risen to a conscious level.) Talk about this artistic expression with someone who cares about you.

Resentment

I try to be a normal, a civilized person
while anger is saved in a vault beneath my heart
In reserve whenever oppression locates me
Anger cloaked within an illusion of harmony
My elated face waiting to attack; from the back,
gossip, innuendo, slander, deceit, and lies
Very indirect, no chance to reveal my disguise
I'm your friend, your confidant, your mate
Cowering before freedom with oppression and hate
Having lost the passion of risk, the courage to
What more of myself would you expect me to give.

Possibilities in Therapy

Here are some of the suggestions from counsellors, psychologists and psychiatrists that over the years have given input into this emotional map.

Phase 1 Frustration Over Time:

Your therapist may explore how much frustration over time has taken its toll on you physically and socially. Multicultural Therapy may be used if your race or culture is responsible for generating negativity in you. In some cases, a person may need psychotropic medication to reduce the symptoms. Person Centered Therapy will be helpful to form a strong trusting therapeutic alliance. Narrative Therapy will be effective to explore your belief system and life events.

Phase 2 Being Stuck:

The therapist may explore those thoughts that are behind you feeling stuck. Cognitive Behavioral Therapy may be used to treat the lack of critical thinking. Existential Therapy may be helpful to expose the illusion of harmony.

Phase 3 Buried Emotions:

The therapist may explore and discover the buried negative feelings. Person-Centered Therapy may be used to form a strong therapeutic alliance. Direct Decision Therapy would be used to explore decision making because decisions are the key to understanding personality. Gestalt Therapy is helpful because it explores the person and his/her relations to the world, and often uses role playing to help with resolution of past conflicts.

Phase 4 Indirect Lashing Out:

A therapist may explore your behavior patterns and the way you indirectly lash out. Anger management and Behavioral Therapy may be helpful to treat aggressive behavior. Relaxation skills would be recommended and if needed Eye Movement Desensitization and Reprocessing (EMDR) would help to alleviate the distress associated with traumatic memories.

Phase 5 Feeling Victimized:

A therapist may like to explore the belief behind your feeling of being a victim of resentment. Values clarification is important in therapy to expose unhelpful beliefs. Existential Therapy may be helpful to expose the inner conflict which may be due to your confrontation with the life problems. Experiential System Therapy brings you back to a more accepting role in the system It helps access your emotions and integrate your mind, body and spirit, and reconnect with your authentic self. In some cases, Assertive Training may be needed to empower people to stand up for themselves.

Phase 6 Accumulating Frustration:

With the help of Narrative Therapy, a therapist may explore the history of how you accumulated frustration time. Narrative therapy may help to identify your values and the skills and knowledge you need to live these values. Direct Decision Therapy would be helpful to understand a person's decision-making regarding his or her dysfunctional behavior. Choice Therapy helps a therapist to understand and treat behavior based on internal motivation.

An Emotional Algorithm for Resentment

Here is an emotional algorithm for resentment. Again, an emotional algorithm is a procedure or formula for solving a possible problem, based on conducting a sequence of specified actions. This is a starting point in helping you regulate your emotions. Talk about this algorithm with someone who cares about you.

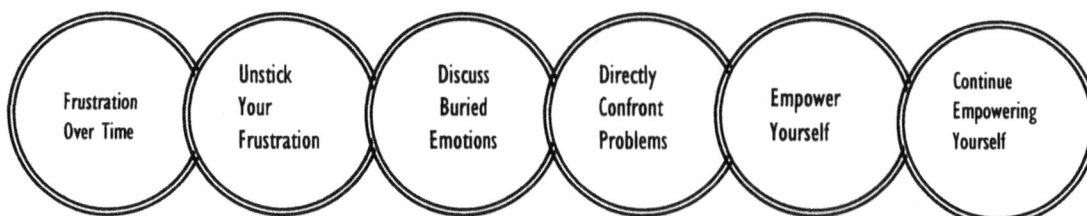

Figure 10.2

Reader's Personalized Algorithm for Resentment

Now it is your turn to give direction to regulating your emotions.

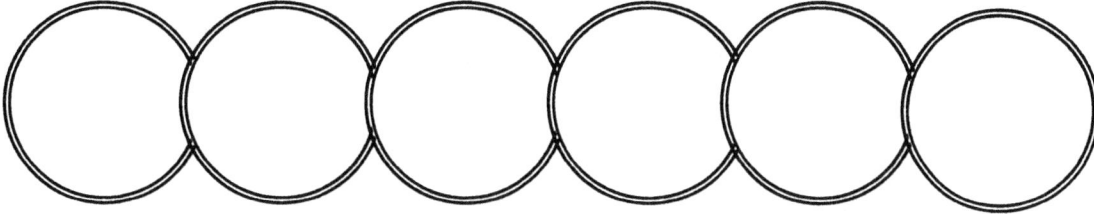

Figure 10.3

Reader's Personalized Action Plan for Emotionally Regulating Resentment.

-
-
-
-
-
-

Chapter 11: Revenge

Introduction

To some, revenge appears as a solution to many problems where individuals feel violated by another, a group or a society. Justification for revenge seems a natural reaction to some people where you want to get even with someone or something. In many cases, the emotion of revenge evolves into a pre-meditated plan based on retaliation. For example, you are hurt by a friend's betrayal. After the hurt has passed, feelings of being violated may grow into a plan to retaliate against that person. For some, revenge is "sweet". Look at the movies presently in your neighborhood theaters. There is bound to be some story devoted to getting someone back for an injustice.

Again, in many acts of revenge where people are violated and are thrown emotionally out of balance, some form of response seems justified. When people retaliate after being violated, the act of "evening the score" seems a natural response, and violence seems an effective alternative to doing just that, "evening the score." Yet, acts of revenge rarely even the score. What is one person's retaliation can become another person's violation, escalating a conflict where violence and retaliation seem more justifiable. How many conflicts have escalated based on this premise?

In this chapter, an attempt is made to develop an emotional algorithm for facing the experience of revenge. The algorithm will talk more about justice than revenge based on the fine line between them. It may be up to you to determine when you develop a plan to get back at someone else whether it is a plan based on revenge or one based on justice. For example, Mothers Against Drunk Driving is a plan based on justice not revenge even though these mothers felt violated by the deaths of their sons and daughters.

Emotional Pattern of Revenge

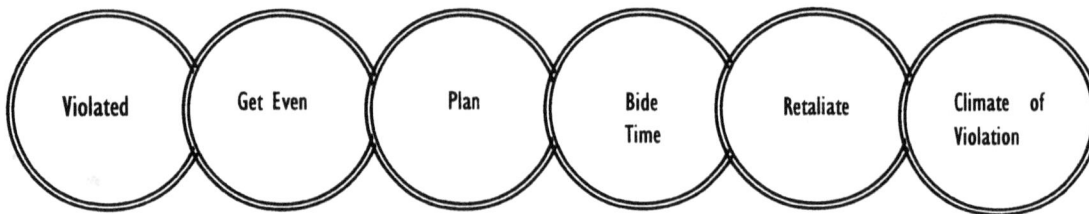

Figure 11.1

Phase 1 Violated:

It is impossible to go through life without feeling violated in some way. For example, you may have been in a relationship and someone left you, or you may have had a job and were let go. These examples and more personal ones such as being injured by another, are violations that you may experience at some point in your life. You may be highly sensitive and feel violated more than others. Or, you may be able to take the violations of others and not let them bother you. It is important to realize that we are all different and sometimes we violate others without even knowing it, or they violate us and do not realize it.

1. What are the certain things in life that make you feel violated?

_____

_____

_____

_____

2. Do you keep thinking about the person(s) or events that made you feel violated?

_____
_____
_____
_____

3. Do you usually get "worked up" just thinking about things that have upset you in the past?

_____
_____
_____
_____

4. After an argument is over, do you usually keep fighting with that person in your mind?

_____
_____
_____
_____

Phase 2 Get Even:

If you have been violated in some way, your body will respond to that violation by having the crisis center in your brain go on alert. Also, when violated you may have a feeling of wanting to get even. That is a natural response to being violated. Remember your brain is already on alert and your feelings are geared towards defending yourself. So, wanting to get even is a natural response. However, how do you want to get even is the question? Some people think getting even is in violating someone back. More accurately, it is your body wanting to get itself emotionally back in balance, and feel the same as before the violation.

1. When was the last time you felt offended and thought of getting even?

_____
_____
_____
_____

2. Do you get frustrated if you could not think of a way to get even with someone who you think deserved it? If so, how do you feel if you couldn't get even with that person?

_____
_____
_____
_____

3. Please write below how you convince yourself that it's alright to get even with people who have wronged you.

_____
_____
_____
_____

4. How often do you re-enact the violation episode in your mind and think about ways to get even with that person (s), group, or system whom you feel have violated you?

_____
_____
_____
_____

Phase 3 Plan:

Here is where you can take charge of your life when someone violates you. At this phase, you can come up with a plan that will eliminate the violation. If you come up with a plan to retaliate and violate the person who violated you, we then call your actions revenge. If you come up with a plan that puts you emotionally back in balance, we call that a plan based on justice. For example, if you want to hurt your father for being a drunk and violating you, then that is a plan based on revenge. If you want to help your father even though he is a drunk and has violated you, and you still want to get him into rehab, then that is a plan based on justice.

1. Do you have a plan to get even with someone who violated you?

_____
_____
_____
_____

2. Do you often daydream about situations where you are getting back at people?

_____
_____
_____
_____

3. Does the imagining of a successful plan give you emotional balance? If so, for how long?

_____
_____
_____
_____

4. Write one of your long living fantasies of revenge if you have any.

_____
_____
_____
_____

Phase 4 Bide Time:

This phase is designated if you choose to retaliate and not clear up the violation. If you have developed a plan to get revenge then you will bide your time waiting to retaliate. Unfortunately, while you bide your time to retaliate you are not doing other important things in your life. In some respects, you are living in the past waiting to make up for violations from the past that still are bothering you. If you are not careful, you may find yourself out of touch with what is going on in the present or what you might want to do in the future. For example, if you ask some people who are feuding what started the feud, many times they cannot even remember what happened.

1. Do you sometimes think the more time that passes, the more satisfaction you are going to get from your revenge?

_____
_____
_____
_____

2. If it applies, what are the important aspects of your life you have been neglecting because you are giving too much of your time and energy to a plan to get even?

_____
_____
_____
_____

3. Do you find it difficult to plan for the present and the future because you are focusing on the past violations?

_____
_____
_____
_____

4. If it applies, are you concerned that by focusing on past violations it could disrupt your plans in some way?

_____
_____
_____
_____

Phase 5 Retaliate:

At this phase, you may get the opportunity to retaliate against the person or persons who have violated you. Some people admit that it feels good to retaliate and for some that is probably correct. Unfortunately, what now might feel good for you has not ended for the person that you retaliated against. He or she may be violated and now may want to come up with a plan, bide their time and retaliate against you. What that means is revenge has become a bigger problem in your life. What was your retaliation has become another's violation and what is another's retaliation will become a further violation?

1. When someone offends you is it difficult for you not to retaliate?

_____
_____
_____
_____

2. Write down the details of the last time you retaliated, if any.

_____
_____
_____
_____

3. Have you ever faced consequences of your retaliation? If so, please explain.

_____
_____
_____
_____

4. Do you sometimes feel that you are caught in a cycle of violation and retaliation?

_____
_____
_____
_____

Phase 6 Climate of Violation:

Now you are living in a climate of violation where you never know when someone will be paying you back for what you did to them. In a way, you are now on alert for when the other person will be getting you back. In some ways, living in a climate of revenge is a violation because you cannot completely relax. In the end, it is better to clear up violations and make yourself at peace than to retaliate and cause future violations. But remember, you do have a right to get even, but only in balancing out yourself.

1. Do you believe that living on alert has taken a toll on your physical and mental health?

_____
_____
_____
_____

2. Do you sometimes get upset with people close to you even though they are not the cause of your frustration?

_____

_____

_____

_____

3. How do you feel afterward when you take out your frustration on innocent people, if relevant?

_____

_____

_____

_____

4. Do you think the climate of revenge is disrupting your everyday life?

_____

_____

_____

_____

Exercises and Activities to Promote Healthy Emotional Response

When people are in a climate of violation and in stress they have difficulty getting perspective of their negative behavior. Therefore, they ignore the ramifications of their revengeful actions. Problem behaviors are hard to change, even when they cause needless suffering. However, changing your behavior can begin when you start to understand why you keep repeating these behaviors even when you truly want to stop.

1. List the cost and benefits of your problem behaviors:

Cost: _____

_____

_____

_____

Benefits: _____

_____

_____

_____

2. Creating Your Own Future: Create a personal mission statement. For example, what would life be like if you were able to care again?

_____

_____

_____

_____

3. The next time you have a disagreement with someone, think about how you acted by filling out the following questions:

        a) The disagreement was about_____

        b) How long did the disagreement last? _____

        c) Did you treat the person with respect? _____

        d) Were you listening carefully to the other person? _____

        e) Did you bring up compromises or solutions to the problem? _____

4. Record your thoughts, feelings, sensations and memories: Keeping track of your thoughts feelings, sensations and memories that cause emotional pain will be helpful to understand your actions and learn if your actions led to positive outcomes or outcomes that caused more pain and suffering. Maintain a journal of:

a) Painful thoughts/Feelings/Sensations/Memories
b) What you did in response?
c) Outcome: Negative or Positive

5. Daily Gratitude: This exercise would help you to turn thoughts outward and feel grateful every day. At the end of each day write down three things you are grateful for. It could be anything. For example, a smile from a stranger, a call from a friend, a morning walk, finding a new recipe, a compliment at work, whatever brightened your day. Write three things you are grateful for right now:

1. _____
2. _____
3. _____

6. Learn self-soothing activities, for example:

a) Mindfulness meditation
b) Nature-walk
4. Calming music
c) Whatever works best for you

7. What does this poem mean to you? It could mean nothing, or it may be a place to start (Express yourself verbally or artistically; write a poem, draw a picture, write a song. Sometimes artistic expression reveals information from our unconscious that has not risen to a conscious level.) Talk about this artistic expression with someone who cares about you.

Revenge

Calm, frozen river in Winter — biding its time
not moving on the surface while the current lies
waiting, expressing itself with peculiar and capricious
force – of cracking ice retaliating against the warm
You remind me of a frozen river with your stare
as cold as ice. Biding your time, eloquent on the surface
while currents of retaliation fight to be the first in line
Tasting the sweetness of ultimate punishment against me

Possibilities in Therapy

Here are some of the suggestions from counsellors, psychologists and psychiatrists that over the years have given input into this emotional map.

Phase 1 Violated:

The therapist may explore your cognitive understanding to deal with the violation. In some cases, medication may be needed. Therefore, Bio-Counseling may be used to understand the neurological brain patterns. Cognitive Behavioral Therapy would be helpful to understand negative thought patterns. Direct Decision Therapy may be helpful to make constructive and positive decisions.

Phase 2 Get Even:

The therapist may use Bio-Counseling to make you understand your feelings of violation and how the amygdale in the brain naturally responds to being violated. Choice Therapy may help you take control of your negative urges to get even. Person Centered Therapy would help to create a strong therapeutic alliance to bring growth and change. In some cases, Eye Movement Desensitization and Reprocessing (EMDR) Therapy may be helpful to recover from a trauma. Meditation and other relaxation skills would be helpful to reduce stress.

Phase 3 Plan:

The therapist may explore your negative thoughts and if you have a plan to violate others. Cognitive Behavioral Therapy would be helpful to recognize and change your negative thoughts. In some cases, conciliation and mediation skills may be used to reach a fair agreement. Solution Focused Therapy may be used to help with your present and future circumstances and goals rather than past experiences.

Phase 4 Bide Time:

Your therapist may explain how inflexible dysfunctional thoughts can cause a lack of emotional and psychological growth. Psychotropic medication would be helpful to reduce symptoms. Eye Movement Desensitization and Reprocessing (EMDR) Therapy could be used to treat inflexible brain pathways. Choice therapy may be used to find a positive plan to get back in emotional balance.

Phase 5 Retaliate:

Your therapist may explain the ramifications of your retaliatory behavior. Group therapy would create significant growth and change. Being with other people who share your experiences would bring comfort and support. Mediation would help to find common ground in a dispute and conciliation would also be helpful to create boundaries to respect in the future.

Phase 6 Climate of Violation:

The therapist may explore your social climate and the reasons behind constant stress violations. Domestic violence is an example of being surrounded by constant violations. In that case, Group Therapy would be helpful. Solution Focused Therapy would help the client to find a safe environment and plan a better future. In some cases, conciliation may be used to break the climate of violence.

An Emotional Algorithm for Revenge

Here is an emotional algorithm for Revenge. Again, an emotional algorithm is a procedure or formula for solving a possible problem, based on conducting a sequence of specified actions. This is a starting point in helping you regulate your emotions. Talk about this algorithm with someone who cares about you.

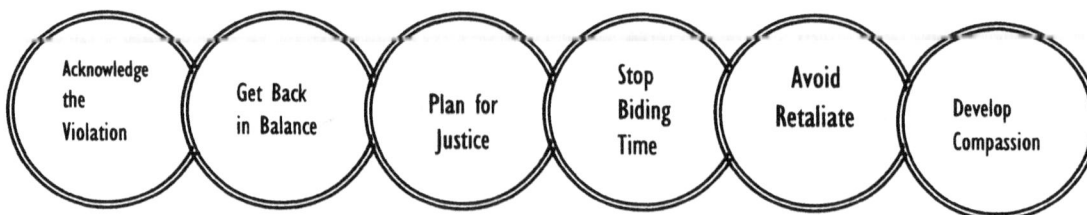

Figure 11.2

Reader's Personalized Emotional Algorithm for Revenge

Now it is your turn to give direction to regulating your emotion

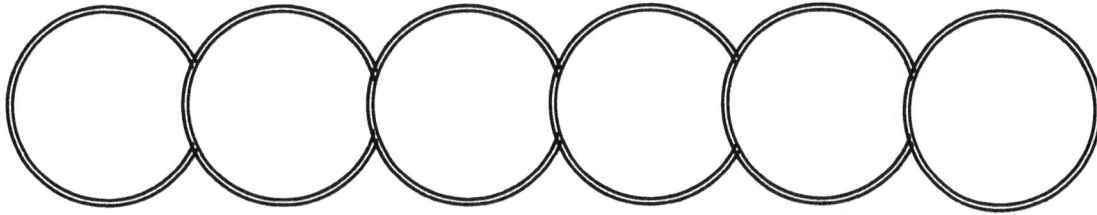

Figure 11.3

Reader's Personalized Action Plan for Emotionally Regulating Revenge.

-
-
-
-
-
-

Chapter 12: Self-Hatred

Introduction

The difficulty with hatred or self-hatred is they usually depict some extreme emotional experience that may not seem possible in everyday life. However, examples of hatred fill our television screens with people rejecting each other in dramatic and sometimes subtle ways. For example, some forms of child abuse may not be physical but can set in motion a pattern of abuse that impacts the abuser and the abused. Or, it may be the indifference displayed when in school a teacher favors certain students at the expense of others. In both cases, some form of rejection takes place where a feeling of being outside the circle is felt. If such an experience is constant and happens in many different circumstances, a pattern may emerge that adds to someone seriously judging their behavior and feelings as unworthy. With time, this can be at the basis of numerous psychological disorders.

Take for example, anorexia nervosa. Someone suffering from this disorder may have rejected their body image no matter how thin he or she has become. Within this disorder, one can find an identity crisis fundamentally based on self-hatred. Another example is conduct disorder where someone hates others to the extent that destroying something seems a logical part of responding in a hateful world. Other times, it is a combination of hating yourself that gives license to hating others. For example, an alcoholic father may hate himself while also abusing his children when drinking alcohol. In these examples, you will find some form of rejection, alienation, condemnation and destruction, and these elements make up the bulk of what is called an emotional pattern of hatred.[1]

As you go through this chapter try to be as open and honest as you can. Very few people want to admit that they hate themselves. It seems too extreme a statement to make when thinking about emotional regulation. However, there are other emotions that seem more plausible and initially help describe your feelings. So, be careful that a pattern of hatred can be under the surface and may eventually get your attention the deeper you go into an exploration of your feelings. Take your time and consider when going through these exercises that the help of a friend or counselor may be in order.

Emotional Pattern of Self-Hatred

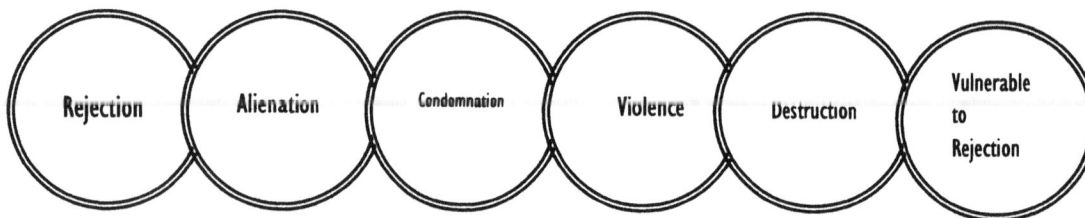

Figure 12.1

Phase 1 Rejection:

Few people want to admit that they hate themselves. If you feel self-hatred it is possible you have gone to great lengths to deny any connection with admitting to feeling this way. That is understandable. To feel hatred toward one's self can be a frightening and lonely experience. If we look at the pattern of self-hatred as an experience instead of a fact, it may be possible to separate one's self from the pattern. Saying it another way, perhaps you do not hate yourself. Maybe you have fallen into a pattern of self-hatred. Maybe deep down inside you love yourself but are unable to admit it. Maybe you cannot admit it because at some point in your life someone rejected you so much that you began to reject yourself. Maybe you got into the habit of rejecting yourself and somewhere along the way began to believe in that rejection. The basis of self-hatred lies in rejection, whether it is rejection within a family, rejection of one's personality, or rejection of one's race. A pattern of self-hatred is less about who you are, and more about how you look at yourself.

1. Do you have a negative opinion of yourself and your future? If so, please write some of your negative opinions about yourself below:

_____
_____
_____
_____

2. Do you over-emphasize what you perceive as your flaws? If so, please list some of your flaws.

_____
_____
_____
_____

3. Do you constantly compare and rate yourself against others? If so, please list some of the qualities that you admire in others and wish you had.

_____
_____
_____
_____

4. Do you reject or deny awareness of positive traits in you?

_____
_____
_____
_____

Phase 2 Alienation:

If for some reason you have rejected yourself, then it would make sense that you would not let people into your life who could further reject you. If you look carefully, you may realize that you may have put up walls to keep others out. Maybe not everyone, but you may keep out enough people who you consider judges of your character. You may feel these walls are necessary to protect yourself against further rejection. Unfortunately, these walls keep you in as much as they keep others out. You may end up isolating yourself from the truth or from others who may be able to give you a more positive interpretation of who you are. You may create the walls to protect yourself from further rejection but in doing so you can cut off chances for further acceptance as well.

1. Do you need people's approval to feel happy and worthwhile? When someone disapproves of you how do you cope with the feelings of rejection?

_____
_____
_____
_____

2. Do you constantly 'mind read' what other people are thinking and feeling about you? If so, what are your concerns?

_____
_____
_____
_____

3. How do you behave when you are around family, friends, or colleagues?

_____
_____
_____
_____

4. Do you constantly compare and rate yourself against others?

_____
_____
_____
_____

Phase 3 Condemnation:

If you have isolated yourself behind your own personal walls, then you are in a perfect position to condemn yourself as a bad person. This is unfortunate because there is a strong likelihood you had nothing to do with being a bad person. For example, is a child who was molested a bad person because later she or he becomes overly sexually active? Or does she or he hate what happened as a child so much that condemning one's self through sexual activity begins to make sense? We believe the second statement is correct. A person experiences self-hatred because of what happened not for being a bad person. Unfortunately, bad-things happen to good people. When you condemn yourself, and take responsibility for what others did to you, then you may end up hating yourself for the actions of others. A healthier approach would be to hate the action that was done to you and not hate yourself. If you have condemned yourself for being a bad person, take a moment and think about whether that is true.

1. What is the trait you most dislike about yourself?

_____
_____
_____
_____

2. Do you get very upset with yourself when you make a mistake? If so, how do you blame yourself?

_____
_____
_____
_____

3. Do you believe people would look down on you if they found out all the mistakes you have made? If so, what do you believe they would think of you?

_____
_____
_____
_____

4. Do you usually blame yourself for the problems in your relationships with other people? If so, what are some of your negative traits causing the problems?

_____
_____
_____
_____

Phase 4 Physical or Psychological Violence:

If you have condemned yourself and you believe it, then some form of physical or psychological violence may take place. The opposite is also true. If you love yourself some form of physical or psychological growth may also take place. What you believe about yourself may influence how you behave. If you believe that you are a bad person then you may begin to act like a bad person. If you believe you are a good person then you will probably try acting like one. Self-hatred is filled with negative beliefs that can make you do terrible things. That does not mean you are terrible person. It means your beliefs are wrong and need to be understood regarding where they come from. This phase may also take the form of *self-sabotage*. Just when you begin to believe good things about yourself, you may take action that will prevent good things from happening to you. For example, you may do things to drive away the people who provide a positive view on your life.

1. Do you often feel upset when people do not meet other people's expectations?

_____
_____
_____
_____

2. Do you usually let people know how you feel when you are upset? Or, maybe not.

_____
_____
_____
_____

3. Have you ever taken your anger out on an innocent person?

_____
_____
_____
_____

4. Have you ever purposefully done something to drive people away from you or to prevent something good from happening in your life?

_____
_____
_____
_____

Phase 5 Destruction:

Physical or psychological violence to yourself leads to destroying yourself in some way. Becoming an alcoholic or not being able to keep a relationship are ways that some self-hatred shows itself in a person's life. If you find yourself destroying or tearing down the good things then check whether a pattern of self-hatred is running your life. Even a simple thing can be an indicator. For example, what happens when someone gives you a compliment? If you cannot accept the compliment it may be because you cannot accept liking yourself? Just remember that self-hatred is a pattern you can fall into and it does not have to define who you are.

1. Have you ever thought you should cut down your drug or alcohol use? Have you ever felt annoyed when people have commented on your use?

_____
_____
_____
_____

2. Do you often feel awkward about praise, and feel relieved when a person changes the topic?

_____
_____
_____
_____

3. Are you satisfied with the person you've turned out to be so far?

_____
_____
_____
_____

4. When was the last time you practiced a self-destructive behavior? If you have.

_____
_____
_____
_____

Phase 6 Vulnerable to Rejection:

We all have had moments of being vulnerable to rejection by others. That does not mean we hate ourselves. However, it may mean we are going through a period in life where certain traumas have made us vulnerable to the rejection of others. Continuing in such a pattern may begin to raise the walls of alienation, condemnation, and self-destruction. Self-hatred destroys many things, the least of which is self-esteem. People who are not self-destructive and do not hate themselves are more likely to cope effectively with rejection from others. Without self-esteem, we become vulnerable to the rejection of others. Self-hatred is a pattern where we can become our own enemy.

1. If you could change one thing about yourself or your life what would it be?

_____
_____
_____
_____

2. Are there specific places, things, or people that may make you hate yourself even more?

_____
_____
_____
_____

3. Do you feel guilty if someone is annoyed with you?

_____
_____
_____
_____

4. Do you feel detached when you are around people?

_____
_____
_____
_____

Exercises and Activities to Promote Healthy Emotional Response

People who suffer from self-hatred may develop an internal voice that is constantly criticizing them and attacking their self-worth. That self-loathing can lead to sabotage and destructive behavior. Some self-help activities and exercises can develop positive inner voices.

1. List the cost and benefits of your behaviors:

Cost: _____
_____
_____

Benefits: _____
_____
_____

2. Write 5 nurturing statements you would like to hear about yourself:

a) _____
b) _____
c) _____
d) _____

3. Recognize and confront your negative judgments. If you are constantly making negative judgments about yourself, you are causing unnecessary suffering. If you often make negative judgments about others you are socially isolating yourself. Follow the example given below and record your judgments and their negative effects on you in a journal.

Judgments about yourself:
  a) Situation
  b) Emotion(s)
  c) Judgment
  d) Magnifying Emotion(s)
  e) Outcome (Negative or Positive)

Judgments about others:
  a) Situation
  b) Emotion(s)
  c) Judgment
  d) Magnifying Emotion(s)
  e) Outcome (Negative or Positive)

4. How do you see yourself and how do others see you?

How do you see yourself? Write down your physical traits, your unique qualities, your greatest abilities and strengths. Write down three words you use to describe your personality and three words you use to describe your relationship toward other people.

_____
_____
_____
_____

How do others see you? Ask someone who knows you well to write down your physical traits, your unique qualities, your greatest abilities, and strengths. Ask them to write three words that come to their mind to describe your personality and three words that come to their mind to describe your relationship toward other people.

_____
_____
_____
_____

5. Imagine your best possible self. Write down a description of your life as you would like to be in five years by imagining the best things that could happen to you.

_____
_____
_____
_____
_____
_____
_____
_____

6. Awe is the feeling of being in the presence of something vast that goes beyond our understanding of the world. Feelings of awe increase our sense of happiness and fulfillment by making us feel that we are connected to others around us. Make a list of experiences that give you feelings of awe.

7. What does this poem mean to you? It could mean nothing, or it may be a place to start (Express yourself verbally or artistically; write a poem, draw a picture, write a song. Sometimes artistic expression reveals information from our unconscious that has not risen to a conscious level.) Talk about this artistic expression with someone who cares about you.

Self-Hatred

Don't bother me
While I drip away
into this pool of
self-doubt
joining the masses
of equivalent ooze
on my way to extinction
in this cauldron of loneliness
Don't save me but if you do,
please tell me who I am

Possibilities in Therapy

Here are some of the suggestions from counselors, psychologists and psychiatrists that over the years have given input into this emotional map.

Phase 1 Rejection:

Your therapist may ask to describe your beliefs in general as well as specific beliefs about rejection. Narrative therapy may be used to explore abuse issues and Existential Therapy can be helpful to explore the inner conflicts and confrontation of the existing problem. Jungian therapy would be helpful to understand who you really are.

Phase 2 Alienation:

A person's feelings of alienation are an important part of a diagnosis. The therapist may help you to build healthy boundaries. Experiential System Therapy may be used to develop healthy interpersonal relationships. Person Centered Therapy may be useful to explore how you perceive yourself. Sensitivity training may also be used if a person struggles with prejudice and has the habit of negative judgments.

Phase 3 Condemnation:

A therapist may explore dysfunctional thoughts related to blaming yourself (i.e. condemnation). Cognitive Behavioral Therapy may be used to recognize a distorted thought process and Rational Emotive Therapy tends to help with amendment of beliefs/thinking in a profound schematic way. In some cases, Solution Focused Therapy may also be used to develop a vision of the future and offer support to determine the skills, resources, and abilities needed to achieve that vision successfully.

Phase 4 Physical or Psychological Violence:

The therapist may explore how a person is violating her or his self. Behavioral Therapy may be used to control the sabotage. Building stress can be controlled by Stress Reduction Training. Cognitive Therapy is helpful to break the cycle of negative self-fulfilling prophecies.

Phase 5 Destruction:

A person's destructive beliefs lead to self-destructive behavior. Cognitive Behavioral Therapy may be used to treat self-rejection. In some cases, crisis counseling becomes essential if a person has suicidal ideation and self-injury issues.

Phase 6 Vulnerable to Rejection:

A therapist may explore your low self-esteem issues. Person Centered Therapy and positive self-regard may help with lower self-esteem. Existential therapy can be helpful with resolving inner conflicts. Narrative Therapy would be helpful to expand a person's focus.

An Emotional Algorithm for Self-Hatred

Here is an emotional algorithm for self-hatred. Again, an emotional algorithm is a procedure or formula for solving a possible problem, based on conducting a sequence of specified actions. This is a starting point in helping you regulate your emotions. Talk about this algorithm with someone who cares about you.

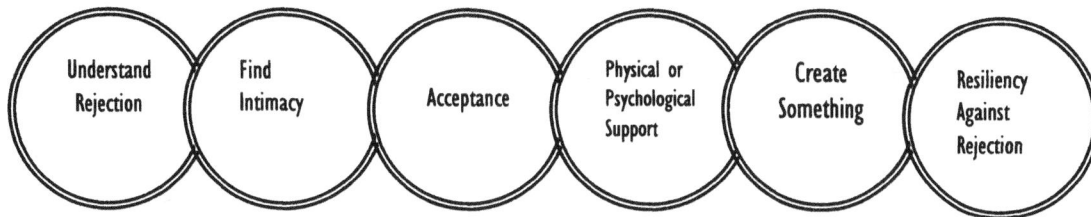

Understand Rejection — Find Intimacy — Acceptance — Physical or Psychological Support — Create Something — Resiliency Against Rejection

Figure 12.2

Reader's Personalized Emotional Algorithm for Self-Hatred

Now it is your turn to give direction to regulating your emotions

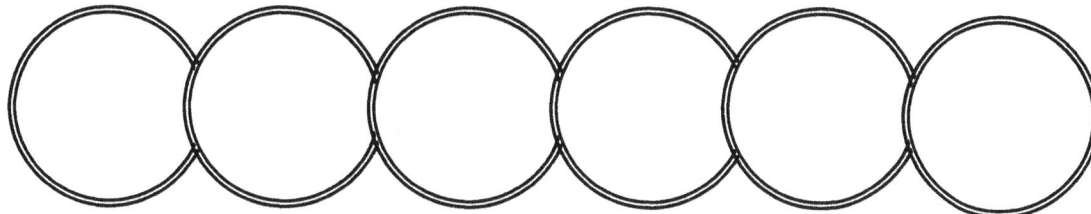

Figure 12.3

Reader's Personalized Action Plan for Emotionally Regulating Self-Hatred.

-
-
-
-
-
-

Notes

1. Information on hatred from a mental health perspective can be found in the following book. Ladd, P.D. & Churchill, A. (2012*), Person-Centered diagnosis and treatment: A model for empowering clients.* London: Jessica Kingsley Publishers. 304–321.

Glossary

Acceptance and Commitment Therapy

Acceptance and Commitment Therapy (ACT) is an empirically based psychological strategy that relies on acceptance and mindfulness strategies, and combines them with commitment and behavior change strategies, to increase a person's ability to be more flexible. Psychological flexibility means living in the present moment more fully, and based on what the situation requires and changing or remaining in the behavior that a person has chosen as valuable. Clients gain the skills to change and accept events in their lives by developing greater clarity about personal values, and commit to needed behavior change (Hayes, Stroshal and Wilson 2003)

Adlerian Therapy

In Adlerian therapy people take responsibility for creating their own destiny, and finding meaning and goals to give their lives a purpose and direction. This allows people to control direction in their lives. The assumption is based on individuals developing a distinctive lifestyle in early childhood, rather than being shaped by childhood experiences. Adlerian Therapy practices a growth model of therapy. It stresses a positive view of human nature that we can control. People start at an early age in creating their own unique style of living and that style stays relatively constant through the remainder of their lives. People are motivated by social interests and how they set goals to face different life tasks (Ferguson 2009).

Anger Management

Anger management refers to the process by which a person learns how to identify stressors, take necessary steps to remain calm, and handle tense situations in a constructive, positive manner. The purpose of anger management is to help a person decrease the heightened emotional and physiological arousal often associated with anger. It is generally impossible to avoid all the people, things, and settings that incite anger, but a person may learn how to control reactions and respond in a socially appropriate manner. The support of a mental health professional may be helpful in this process.

Art Therapy

Art therapy is the therapeutic use of art making, within a therapeutic relationship by people who experience illness, trauma, or challenges in living, and by people who seek personal development. Through creating art and reflecting on the art products and processes, people can increase awareness and be more aware of others. Such awareness helps people enjoy the life-affirming pleasures of making art while coping with symptoms, stress, and traumatic experiences (Burt 2011).

Assertiveness Training

Assertiveness training is a form of behavior therapy designed to help people stand up for themselves—to empower themselves, in more contemporary terms. Assertiveness is a response that seeks to maintain an appropriate balance between passivity and aggression.

Attachment Focused Family Therapy

The goal of AFFT is to provide families with an opportunity to safely become engaged with their therapist, along with the possibility of a primary attachment figure, across a full range of experiences. By therapeutically connecting with families, the therapist's goal is for each family member to become more aware of self, which was previously not open to them. The inter-subjective experiences with the family, allows them to explore the traumatic and shameful events of the past. The therapist provides family members with new meaning to events so that they can more fully understand the narrative of their family history (Hughes 2011).

Behavioral Therapy

Behavior therapy based on the assumption that emotional problems are learned responses to the environment, and that these dysfunctional behaviors can be unlearned. From the perspective of behavioral therapists, the reasons behind behaviors are not as important as that we can changes these behaviors. Some examples of behavioral therapy techniques include systematic desensitization and operant conditioning (Herkov 2006).

Cognitive Therapy

Cognitive therapy is based on the belief that the way we think about things affects how we feel emotionally. Cognitive therapy focuses on present thinking, behavior, and communication rather than on past experiences and is oriented toward problem solving. Cognitive therapy is sometimes called cognitive behavior therapy because it aims to help people in the ways they think (the cognitive) and in the ways, they act (the behavior) (Leahy 2003).

Cognitive Behavioral Therapy

A form of psychotherapy that integrates theories of cognition and learning with treatment techniques derived from cognitive therapy and behavioral therapy. CBT assumes that cognitive, emotional, and behavioral variables are functionally interrelated. Treatment is aimed at identifying and modifying problematic behaviors through cognitive restructuring and behavioral techniques to achieve change (Beck 1995).

Cognitive Processing Theory

Cognitive Processing Therapy (CPT) is an evidenced-based manualized treatment protocol that has been found effective for the treatment of posttraumatic stress disorder (PTSD) and other corollary symptoms following traumatic events. It focuses on how the traumatic event is construed and coped with by a person who is trying to regain a sense of mastery and control in his or her life. Typically conducted as a 12 sessions protocol with a recommended follow-up session around 30 days after the end of treatment, it helps to consider the overall therapy in terms of phases of treatment.

Conciliation Training

Traditionally, conciliation has meant the process by which disputing people are brought together to talk about their conflict. This concept of "bringing together" to include not only the process by which people are literally brought together in the same room, but also the way they are brought together psychologically so they can move beyond hostility, suspicions, and avoidance to address the disputes that divide them. The primary focus of conciliation is building or rebuilding a relationship so that the disputing people themselves can agree to address their differences (Ladd 2005).

Crisis Counseling

A crisis refers not just to a traumatic event or experience, but to an individual's response to the situation. The events that trigger this crisis can run the gamut of life experience, from developmental hurdles (such as going through puberty) to natural disasters to the death of a loved one. Crisis counseling is an intervention that can help individuals deal with the crisis by offering assistance and support.

Critical Incident Stress Debriefing

Critical Incident Stress Debriefing is a process that prevents or limits the development of post-traumatic stress in people exposed to critical incidents. Professionally conducted debriefings help people cope with, and recover from an incident's after effects. CISD enables participants to understand that they are not alone in their reactions to a distressing event, and provides them with an opportunity to discuss their thoughts and feelings in a controlled, safe environment. Optimally, CISD occurs within 24 to 72 hours of an incident. However, it must be noted that telling one's traumatic story should be preceded with some form of trauma stabilization (Kinchin 2007).

Dialectical Behavioral Therapy (DBT)

Dialectical behavior therapy provides training in mindfulness meditation to foster improvements in tolerating one's feelings. It has been successfully demonstrated to reduce self-mutilation and suicidal behavior in chronically suicidal patients with borderline personality disorder. Dialectical behavioral therapy (DBT) aims to help people to validate their emotions and behaviors, examine those behaviors and emotions that have a negative impact on their lives, and make a conscious effort to bring about positive changes (McKay, Wood and Brantley 2007).

Direct Decision Therapy

Considers that the individual, although largely a product of his genes and environment, still is able to exert a certain amount of choice, and that personality is the integration of these factors. Methods by which the therapist may intervene are noted; E.g., drugs, and removal of the patient from their environment. The therapist may also teach the patient alternative methods of responding to their environment. It is noted that there are sometimes advantages to feeling anxious, and that the therapist must understand the goals of his patient. "decision therapy rests on a deep-seated belief in the inherent strength of the human being no matter how troubled. It sees man not as a victim, but as capable of exercising some degree of freedom within the framework of his biology and his society." (PsycINFO Database Record (c) 2016 APA, all rights reserved)

Eye Movement Desensitization Reprocessing (EMDR)

EMDR uses a patient's own rapid, rhythmic eye movements. These eye movements dampen the power of emotionally charged memories of past traumatic events. In EMDR, a patient brings to mind emotionally unpleasant images and beliefs about themselves related to their traumatic event. With these thoughts and images in mind, patients are asked to also pay attention to an outside stimulus, such as eye movements or finger tapping guided by the therapist (Mailberger 2009).

Existential Therapy

A kind of psychotherapy that promotes self-awareness and personal growth by stressing current reality and by analyzing and altering specific patterns of response to help a person realize his or her potential. The existential psychotherapist is generally not concerned with the client's past; instead, the emphasis is on the choices to be made in the present and future. The counselor and the client may reflect upon how the client has answered life's questions in the past, but attention ultimately shifts to searching for a new and increased awareness in the present and enabling a new freedom and responsibility to act (May 1994).

Exposure/Response Therapy

Exposure therapy is an effective behavioral treatment for a variety of anxiety disorders including OCD. Exposure therapy works by taking advantage of a natural process called habituation. Habituation is a form of learning whereby a person will stop responding or paying attention to a stimulus such as a thought, object, place, people or action with repeated exposure. Exposure therapy works by creating opportunities for the patient to unlearn dangerous or threatening associations (Rosqvist 2005).

Family Systems Therapy

A type of psychotherapy designed to identify family patterns that contribute to a behavior disorder or mental illness and help family members break those habits. Family therapy involves discussion and problem-solving sessions with the family. Some of these sessions may be as a group, in couples, or one on one. A therapist or team of therapists conducts multiple sessions to help families deal with issues that may interfere with the functioning of the family and the home environment (Datillio 2010).

Gestalt Therapy

According to gestalt therapy, context affects experience, and a person cannot be fully understood without understanding his or her context. With this in mind, gestalt psychotherapy recognizes that no one can be purely objective—including therapists whose experiences and perspectives are also influenced by their own contexts—and practitioners accept the validity and truth of their clients' experiences.

Group Therapy

Group therapy is a form of psychosocial treatment where a small group of patients meet regularly to talk, interact, and discuss problems with each other and the group leader (therapist). Group therapy attempts to give individuals a safe and comfortable place where they can work out problems and emotional issues. Clients gain insight into their own thoughts and behavior, and offer suggestions and support to others. In addition, clients who have a difficult time with interpersonal relationships can benefit from the social interactions that are a basic part of the group therapy experience (Brabender, Smolar and Fallon 2004).

Jungian Therapy

Jung believed that the personal unconscious is only the top layer of a much deeper, larger collective unconscious - the uncontrollable, inherited part of the human psyche which is made up of patterns (archetypes) common to all humanity. In Jungian therapy, these patterns can explain why we have habits we cannot break, such as addictions, depression and anxiety. Therefore, the approach aims to analyze these archetypes in order to better understand the human self. Through the process of self-awareness, transformation and actualization, Jungian therapy can help individuals see what is out of balance in their psyche. This is to empower them to consciously make changes that will help them to become more balanced and whole.

Mindfulness Therapy

Mindfulness in contemporary psychology is an approach to increasing awareness and skillful responding to mental processes that contributes to emotional distress and maladaptive behavior. Mindfulness approaches are not considered relaxation or mood management techniques, but a form of mental training to reduce cognitive vulnerability to reactive modes of mind that might otherwise heighten stress and emotional distress, or that may otherwise perpetuate psychopathology (Seigel 2010).

Multi-Cultural Counseling

Multicultural counseling is defined as what occurs when the professional counselor works with a client from a different cultural group, and how that might affect interactions that take place within the counseling relationship. This definition is expanded to include dissimilarities in religion and spirituality, sexual orientation, gender, age and maturity, socioeconomic class, family history, and even geographic location. The first step in effective multicultural counseling is to identify and acknowledge these differences between the counselor and client.

Narrative Therapy

The basic concept of narrative therapy is that our personal identities are formed by the accounts of our life experiences that are found in our personal narratives or stories that we tell about ourselves. The responsibility of the narrative therapist involves being interested in assisting the client with their lifestyles and stories as well as any possibilities that are associated with those experiences. At the same time, the therapist will investigate the client's problems and how they have influenced their lives. Narrative therapy approaches contend that a person's identity is primarily shaped by these narratives or stories of their lives whether they are culturally genuine or uniquely personal in nature (Madigan 2010).

Neuro-Linguistic Programming

NLP explores the relationships between how we think (neuro), how we communicate (linguistic) and our patterns of behavior and emotion (programs). Neurolinguistic programming (NLP) is aimed at enhancing the healing process by changing the conscious and subconscious beliefs of patients about themselves, their illnesses, and the world. These limiting beliefs are "reprogrammed" using a variety of techniques drawn from other disciplines including hypnotherapy and psychotherapy (Burton and Ready 2010).

Person-Centered Therapy

Person-centered therapy, which is also known as client-centered, non-directive, or Rogerian therapy, is an approach to counseling and psychotherapy that places much of the responsibility for the treatment process on the client, with the therapist taking a nondirective role. It is a non-directive approach to therapy. "Directive" meaning any therapist behavior that deliberately steers the client's behavior, instead of letting the client find direction for his or her own behavior, the client is empowered to find the experience that fits the meaning in their life. (Rogers and Kramer 2007).

Psychodynamic Therapy

A type of psychotherapy that draws on psychoanalytic theory to help people understand the roots of emotional distress, often by exploring unconscious motives, needs, and defenses. A therapeutic approach that assumes dysfunctional or unwanted behavior is caused by unconscious, internal conflicts and focuses on gaining insight into these motivations. The approach assumes everyone has an unconscious/subconscious mind that often holds on to feelings that are too difficult to face (McWilliams, 2004).

Psychotropic Drug Therapy (Bio-Counseling)

Psycho-pharmacotherapy (Psychotropic Drug Therapy) is the use of medications in the treatment of psychiatric disorders. These medications are frequently referred to as psychoactive or psychotropic medications. The medications used in psycho-pharmacotherapy are usually prescription medications. There are five major classifications of therapeutic psychoactive/psychotropic medications commonly used in the treatment of psychiatric disorders; anti-psychotic, anxiolytic sedatives (anxiety reduction), antimanic agents (mania reduction), antidepressants, psychostimulants (alertness for example ADHD) (Mrazek 2010).

Rational Emotive Therapy

Rational emotive behavior therapy's (REBT) central premise is that events alone do not cause a person to feel depressed, enraged, or highly anxious. Rather, it is one's beliefs about the events which contribute to unhealthy feelings and self-defeating behaviors. Rational emotive behavior therapy teaches the client to identify, evaluate, dispute, and act against his or her irrational self- defeating beliefs, thus helping the client to not only feel better but to get better. It is an active-directive, solution-oriented therapy which focuses on resolving emotional, cognitive and behavioral problems in clients (Ellis 2007).

Reality Therapy (Choice Theory)

Reality therapy attempts to help people control the world around them more effectively so that they are better able to satisfy their needs. Clients seek to discover what they really want and whether what they are currently doing (how they are choosing to behave) is actually bringing them nearer to, or further away from, that goal. Reality Therapy is a considered a cognitive-behavioral approach to therapy; that is, it focuses on facilitating the client to become aware of, and if necessary, change, his/her thoughts and actions (Glasser 2001).

Solution Based Therapy

Solution-focused brief therapy targets what works rather than what's wrong. It is based on a non-pathology model that emphasizes the strengths and resources of client(s) in a collaborative effort to reach goals and resolve problems rapidly. It focuses on treatment directed to the active resolution of personality or behavioral problems rather than to the speculative analysis of the unconscious. It usually concentrates on a specific problem or symptom and is limited to a specified number of sessions with the therapist (Bertolino 2009).

Stress Reduction Techniques

Stress is the body's normal response to anything that disturbs its natural physical, emotional, or mental balance. Secondary biochemical stress comes from an imbalance in your body that occurs because of prolonged mental stress. Stress reduction refers to various strategies that counteract this response and produce a sense of relaxation and tranquility. Meditation and other forms of relaxation such as yoga are recommended as stress reduction techniques (Davis *et al.* 2008).

Suicide Ideation

Suicidal ideation is a common medical term for thoughts about suicide. Thoughts may be fleeting in nature, or they may persist and resolve into a formulated plan. Many people who experience suicidal thoughts do not die by suicide, although they may exhibit suicidal behavior or make suicide attempts. People who find themselves experiencing suicidal thoughts or behaviors may find that they do so as a result of conditions such as depression, hopelessness, severe anxiety, insomnia, or panic attacks. Not all people who are diagnosed with these or other medical or mental health conditions will experience suicidal ideation, but some may.

Bibliography

Battaglia, Sofia. 2016. *Overcoming Jealous: A Guided Workbook.* Amazon Digital Services

Beck, Judith. 1995. *Cognitive Therapy: Basics and Beyond.* New York, NY: The Guilford Press.

Bertolino, Bob. 2009. The Therapist's Notebook on Strengths and Solution-Based Therapies: Homework, Handouts and Activities. London, UK: Routledge Publishers.

Bevan, Lynda. 2009. *Life Without Jealousy: A Practical Guide.* New York, NY: Loving Healing Press.

Blanchfield, Kyle and Peter Ladd 2013. *Leadership, Violence and School Climate: Case Studies in Creating Non-violent Schools.* Lanham, MD: Rowman & Littlefield Education.

Bradbender, Virginia, Andrew, Smolar, April Fallon. *Essentials of Group Therapy.* New York, NY: Wiley.

Burt, Hellen. 2011. *Art Therapy and Postmodernism.* London, UK: Jessica Kingsley Publishers.

Burton, Kate, and Romillia Ready. 2010. Neuro-Linguistic Programming for Dummies. Hoboken, NJ: John Wiley & Sons Inc.

Dattilio, Frank, M. 2010. The Family Therapy Treatment Planner. Hoboken, NJ: Wiley Publications.

Davis, Martha., Elizabeth, Eshelman, Mathew McKay, M. 2008. The Relaxation & Stress Reduction Workbook. Oakland, CA: New Harbinger Press

Ellis, Albert. and Windy, Dryden. 2007. The Practice of Rational Emotive Therapy. New York: NY: Springer Publishing.

Ferguson, Edward, D. 2009. Adlerian Theory: An Introduction. North Charleston, SC: Book Surge LLC

Frankl, Viktor 2000 *Man's Search for Ultimate Meaning.* New York, NY: Basic Books.

Glasser, W. 2001. *Counseling with Choice Theory.* New York, NY: Harper Paperback

Herkov, Michael. 2006. 'About Behavior Therapy.' *Psych Central.* Retrieved on August 20, 2011, .

Hughes, Daniel, A. 2011. Attachment-Focused Family Therapy Workbook. New York, NY: W. W. Norton and Company.

Kierkegaard, Soren. 2009. *Works of Love.* New York, NY: Harper Perennial Modern Classics

Kinchin, David. 2007. *A Guide to Psychological Debriefing: Managing Emotional Decompression and Post-Traumatic Stress Disorder.* London, UK: Jessica Kingsley Publishers.

Ladd, Peter, D. 2005. *Mediation, Conciliation and Emotions: A Practitioner's Guide for Understanding Emotions in Dispute Resolution.* Lanham, MD: University Press of America.

———, 2007. Relationships and Patterns of Conflict Resolution: A Reference Book for Couple's Counselors. Lanham, MD: University Press of America.

———, 2009. Emotional Addictions: A Reference Book for Addictions and Mental Health Counseling. Lanham, MD: University Press of America.

Ladd, Peter, D. and Ann Marie Churchill. 2012. *Person-Centered Diagnosis and Treatment in Mental Health: A Model for Empowering Clients.* London, UK: Jessica Kingsley Publisher

Ladd, Peter D. and Kyle, E Blanchfield. 2016. *Mediation, Conciliation, and Emotions: The Role of Emotional Climate in Understanding Violence and Mental Illness,* Revised Edition. Lanham, MD: Lexington Books.

Leahy, Robert, L. 2003. *Cognitive Techniques: A Practitioner's Guide.* New York, NY: Guilford Press.

Madigan, Stephen. 2010. Narrative Therapy (Theories of Psychotherapy). Washington, DC: American Psychological Association.

McKay, Mathew, Jeffery Wood, and Jeffery, Brantley. 2007. *Dialectical Behavior Therapy Skills Workbook: Practical DBT Exercises for Learning Mindfulness, Interpersonal Effectiveness, Emotion Regulation & Distress Tolerance.* Oakland, CA: New Harbinger Publications.

McWilliams, Nancy. 2004. Psychodynamic Psychotherapy: A Practitioner's Guide. New York, NY: The Guilford Press.

Mrazek, David. 2010). *Psychiatric Pharmacogenomics.* Oxford, UK: Oxford University Press.

Moustakas, Clark 1994. *Phenomenological Research Methods.* Thousand Oaks, CA: Sage Publishing

Piaget, Jean 1972. *Structuralism.* New York, NY: Harper & Row.

Robbie-Gill, Alain, Richard Howard, *Tom McCarthy.* 2012. *Jealousy.* London, UK: Alma Classic LTD.

Rogers, Carl. 1978. *Carl Rogers on Personal Power: Inner Strength and its Revolutionary Impact.* London, UK: Trans-Atlantic Publications.

Rogers, Carl. and Peter Kramer. 1995. On Becoming a Person: A Therapist's View of Psychotherapy. New York, NY: Mariner Books

Siegel, Daniel, J. 2010. *The Mindful Therapist: A Clinician's Guide to Mindsight and Neural Integration.* New York, NY: W. W. Norton and Company.

Siegel, Daniel, J. 2016. *Mind.* New York, NY: W. W. Norton and Company.

White, Gregory and Paul Mullen. 1989. *Jealousy: Theory, Research and Strategies.* New York, NY, US: Guilford Press.

About the Author and Contributor

Author:

Peter D. Ladd PhD has been a tenured faculty member at St. Lawrence University in the Graduate School of Education for over thirty years. He coordinates the Mental Health Counseling Program, and has worked for thirty-five years in St. Lawrence University's satellite graduate school program on the Akwesasne Mohawk Reservation. Over his career, he has written ten books, one of them winning a national book award. He has written numerous articles in the areas of addictions counseling, mental health counseling, relationship counseling, and conflict resolution. Dr. Ladd worked on the Akwesasne Mohawk Reservation for twenty five years where he established two mental health counseling centers and was the licensed clinical supervisor for the Tekanikonrahwa:kon Holistic Health and Wellness Program. He is a strong environmentalist and was President of Save the River (St. Lawrence River) in Clayton, NY.

Contributor:

Yasmeen R. Zaidi has a Master's of Science in Mental Health Counseling from Saint Lawrence University. She also has a Master's in Art & Design from University of Peshawar. She worked as an interior design consultant in Pakistan for several years. She uses a dynamic and strengths-based approach to counseling. She likes to create a safe space for her clients to share their unique; stories, resiliency strategies, and growth potential. She respects cultural diversity and specializes in multicultural counseling. She believes in humanistic approaches to mental health counseling, spirituality and east-west psychology. She contributed to the cultural research in the book *Mediation, Conciliation, and Emotions: The Role of Emotional Climate in Understanding Violence and Mental Illness* by Peter D. Ladd and Kyle Blanchfield. 2016. Lexington Books. She supports the arts in her own community and is a member of Cinema 10, a volunteer group that presents alternative film programming and is a non-profit supported by the New York State Council on the Arts.

www.ingramcontent.com/pod-product-compliance
Lightning Source LLC
Chambersburg PA
CBHW051425290326
41932CB00048B/3231